teaching languages
to adults

teaching languages
to adults

Edited by Duncan Sidwell

Centre for Information on Language Teaching and Research

First published 1984
Copyright © 1984 Centre for Information on Language
Teaching and Research
ISBN 0 903466 72 4
Printed in Great Britain by Multiplex Techniques Ltd
Published by Centre for Information on Language Teaching
and Research, 20 Carlton House Terrace, London SW1Y 5AP

CONTENTS

PREFACE

This short book seeks to do three things –

- to give a presentation and analysis of the needs of the adult student;
- to advise about how these needs may be met;
- to discuss the roles and needs of the people most concerned with teaching, in-service education and organisation.

One of the significant and regrettable facts about modern languages in adult education is the relative isolation of tutors and the lack of strong formal structures for their support, though this, naturally, varies from area to area and from centre to centre. What this volume seeks to do therefore is to offer general principles for teaching and organising which may help to bridge some of the gaps which exist in experience and organisation. For many reasons the questions facing tutors and organisers cannot be dealt with in isolation. The type of course which is offered, the publicity, the methodology and the organisation are inter-related as the chapters in this book make clear, and it is important that a common understanding should form the basis for discussion between those who are teaching and those who are concerned with organising.

It is hoped that this volume will go some way towards achieving this common understanding.

DUNCAN SIDWELL

MODERN LANGUAGES AND THE ADULT STUDENT

David Smith

This chapter will be concerned with the motivation of adults joining evening classes and will attempt to describe ways in which teachers should adjust to the needs of adult learners. It will have in mind the adult who joins a non-vocational evening class, in the more commonly taught European languages, under the normal pattern of evening class organisation. It will look only in passing at the needs of the more specialised learners.

According to the Russell Report (1), between 80% - 90% of the classes offered in the typical evening centre are accounted for by domestic subjects, physical activities, arts and crafts, music and drama, foreign languages, and practical activities such as woodwork and car maintenance, with the remainder being made up by some others of the more 'academic' subjects.

Of the subjects regarded as 'academic' in schools, foreign languages are by far the most popular in evening classes. If they jostle for importance with the above cluster of rather practical subjects, this may tell us something of the motivation of the students who enrol for the classes. I shall return to this point later. The continuing popularity of foreign languages amongst adults is encouraging, and is a fairly long established phenomenon. In Leicestershire, for instance, something between 8% - 10% of all the evening classes advertised annually are in foreign languages. In a count, a survey of some of the most popular evening classes locally showed the following:

Subject	Number of classes	Total number of students
Keep fit	152	3,542
Yoga	152	3,352
All modern foreign languages	208	3,241
Dress-making	225	3,214
Art	151	2,499
Handicrafts	161	2,247
Dancing	65	2,036

In all, the survey showed 2,631 classes, in 124 subjects. Modern foreign languages provided 8% of the total number of courses.

1

It is worth noting that the demand remains high. Although today the great majority of children begin a foreign language (usually French) during their school course, it is interesting to note that French remains with German the most popular evening class language, and that the majority of advertised evening classes are aimed at beginners. Radio and television broadcasts also aim particularly at beginners. This suggests that many people begin a foreign language more than once in their life. Indeed, it is not uncommon for some adult learners to return for several years in succession to the same beginners' class, with the same teachers. Certainly, a relatively small proportion of those who begin in one year return to a slightly more advanced class the following year. Colin Harding (2) found that of all the students enrolled in first year language classes in a particular survey, 58% did not intend to return for a further course later. Duncan Sidwell's survey (3) confirmed this, only 38.7% of the students involved having previously attended evening classes in languages.

DROPOUT

Given the apparent popularity of foreign language classes, at least as far as their availability is concerned, it is interesting to examine a related phenomenon, that of student dropout. By 'dropout' here is meant students who leave a course for good, before the end of the period for which it is due to run. There is an extensive literature on dropout, some of which is surveyed by Roberts and Webb (4). Most of this literature applies to vocational classes, which often lose rather high proportions of their students, as do some of the more academic classes. Useful information on dropout from non-vocational classes can be found in Adult education - adequacy of provision (5). This showed that 11% of the student sample examined had not completed a course in which they had previously enrolled. The small sample of classes investigated by Roberts and Webb (394 classes at four centres over two years) showed a dropout of 15.5% of all enrolments in all subjects. In the case of language classes, the dropout was 16%. It may be, then, that language classes lose a rather higher proportion of students through dropout than other classes. Duncan Sidwell's survey (3) confirms the relative figures. Whereas the dropout from 131 non-language classes (2,335 students enrolled) was 28.3%, the dropout from 63 language classes (1,000 students enrolled) was 34.7%.

It is difficult to know exactly what dropout indicates. If at the end of a course students decide not to enrol for a second year (see Harding above) it may be that they have got from the course all that they wanted. Even some students, in some subjects, may feel this if they leave before the end of a course. However, a higher than average dropout during a course is alarming. Students are often too polite to give totally honest reasons for why they drop out, and often say that their domestic or business commitments make it hard for them to continue with the class. But it is not clear why these commitments should be more onerous than the average in the case of language classes.

WHO ARE THE STUDENTS?

Presumably an understanding of the above phenomenon would lead to higher satisfaction and lower dropout rate among students. What do we know about adult students? As a good number of the teachers who take adult evening classes are also school teachers, an attempt to answer that question might profitably also include a consideration of some of the ways in which classes of adult students differ from classes of children.

1) Interest in education is known to be related to social class. The social classes most prominently represented in adult education groups are those classified by the Registrar General as C1 - C3, with C3 most evident. This group includes middle and lower ranking professional people, who are twice as prominent in adult classes as in the population as a whole. In the NIAE Survey (5) only one third of the students attending evening classes who were interviewed had not previously had some form of education since leaving school.

2) This suggests an inherent interest in education for its own sake. Furthermore, many adults attending classes are rate payers, helping to finance the school system, and virtually all of them pay a fee to join the class. This suggests some positive motivation to learn. Motivation is a critical factor in learning, and can make fast progress possible.

3) The largest age group represented in adult education classes generally is that of the 18 - 34 years old. The NIAE Survey (5) puts the proportion at 44%, with about three times as many women as men on the register. This will not be true of many classes, but it represents a general picture, although Sidwell's survey of language classes (3) shows the sexes to be more evenly balanced than is the case when all courses are considered.

Unlike a typical children's class, the adult class may contain a very wide age range. It has long been accepted that language learning ability declines with age, but this view is being increasingly challenged. Burstall, and Carroll, (quoted by Hawkins in Baer (6)) both suggest that contact time is a more reliable single predictor of success in language learning than age, and Hawkins also quotes Swedish evidence that adults may actually acquire a comprehension ability faster than children. In terms of raw hours, of course, adults have far less contact with the language in class than school pupils.

4) Unlike school pupils, adults opt into language classes and as we

3

have seen, they express a numerically strong demand for them. It is fairly easy to guess why foreign language classes are popular with adults. Ever more people take holidays abroad. Some people also find that increasing commercial contacts abroad make it potentially useful to be able to speak a foreign language. Some, who need to acquire a high degree of fluency quickly, enrol in specialist classes, but some, with less specific needs, join evening classes. Some adults are 'just interested' in languages, others are interested in finding out what language learning is like. Others are interested in foreign countries and hope that they will learn something of them by joining a foreign language class. Colin Harding (2), in his survey conducted in Manchester, found these broad categories of reasons expressed for joining a foreign language class:

Holiday interests	33%
'Pure interest' in languages	25%
Business/professional	15%
Other reasons	27%

Harding's survey was on the basis of a rather small sample, but his figures tally very closely with those reported by Sidwell (3), who also suggests that the holiday interest may account for the relatively high number of couples who join evening classes together.

The category of 'other reasons' includes all sorts of motivations, from parents who want to learn French because their children are doing so at school, through the couples who have joined because one has urged the other to come, the person who actually wants an evening away from the family and home, and retired teachers anxious to keep their brains active, to the elderly person who needs company, to keep warm, and to do something different from what they did on the same evenings last year. It may well be a category which includes some people who cannot actually say very clearly why they have enrolled.

Thus student motivations are mixed. The vocational interest was shown in the NIAE survey (5) to be about 10% overall, in students attending non-vocational classes. But this vocational element often seems to fuse with motives relating to personal enrichment or self-development. In the NIAE survey (5) over 40% of the students thought that this was their main motive: 'an insatiable desire to learn, even though I am now too old for any specialist knowledge to be of any material benefit financially', as one students put it (in Rogers's (7)). Many people want to stretch themselves, intellectually or practically, through an educational activity.

Related to this, there is a similar motive, which is that of testing oneself against what is perceived as a potentially difficult task, strengthening one's own confidence and perhaps satisfying an interest in something long considered as esoteric and demanding. 'If they could do 'O' level French, it would prove something to themselves and to their families' (tutor, quoted by Rogers (7)). This makes it the more sad if some people drop out from language classes for reasons perhaps not totally related to the difficulty of the subject. Over 10% of the NIAE sample gave social reasons for joining a class, and it is important to accept that adult education serves a social purpose in addition to a purely academic one: in fact, the small proportion of 'academic' classes suggests that academic motivations are rather restricted. Michael Hay (8) makes this important point well. 'Having to fit in with a group for a common purpose (languages or not) and having to contribute enough to make a social as well as a learning success of this group – in the middle of life – is one of the mentally healthy and most educative things one can do for oneself... often, tutors are fully aware of the exhilaration of this experience – I am sure I get as much out of it as my students do – hence, the high degree of dedication shown by so many in this field.'

The social motive can be of help at times, because people anxious to make friends, for example, will tend to be anxious to get to know the other members of the class, and may be willing to help organise activities for the group as a whole. Often, needing the security of the group, they will also work hard, so as to remain a respected member of it. 'When my wife died... my whole way of life became geared to a second education and I pride myself that I have become an expert on eighteenth century silver, a fluent speaker of bad Spanish and an interested spectator of the arts' (quoted in Rogers (7)). In the context of non-vocational adult education, all motivations are legitimate, even desirable. However, teachers need to appreciate the differing types of student motivation. In any given evening class, it is unsafe to assume that all the students are there because they have a strong desire to learn the language. In centres which are large enough to run several classes in any one language, it may be possible to organise courses with different aims, and this might increase the motivational homogeneity of the group, at least superficially. But in many cases, the mixed nature of the group motivations will remain. In these cases, the teacher's organisation of the class will need to take account of the various interests and hopes. This being so, it is clearly a good idea for the first session of the class to include some discussion of what pupils hope they will get from their course. This will put the teacher at the very least into a more realistic position towards the students. It will also allow the teacher to begin to define the students' needs. These may be, and often are different from their vaguely – or even less vaguely – expressed ambitions, and will be examined later.

5) Just as motivations are mixed, so is the range of attainment in many adult classes, even at the beginning and even in classes billed as being for beginners. Many adults have somehow been in contact with the language previously, perhaps at school, perhaps on holiday,

perhaps by attempting to follow a broadcast or recorded course. In Sidwell's survey (3), 51% of French level one students were re-beginners. Coupled with mixed language learning aptitudes, this rapidly produces mixed ability groups. In larger centres again, it may be possible to do some form of setting according to ability, but this is not always possible.

Furthermore, as a result of the greater experience resulting from increased years, and the experience of having tinkered with the language before, or perhaps of having learnt another language at school, adults bring certain expectations to the class with them. Some will probably expect the group to be taught predominantly in the full class mode, with the emphasis on formal grammar, and perhaps with a good deal of the lesson conducted in English: they may well expect to be asked to learn again in the same way as that by which they may have failed to learn a language successfully at school, blaming themselves for such failure rather than the method employed, or the teacher involved. As a result, some may be resistant to less traditional approaches. Others, of course, having attended evening classes in other subjects, may expect a pleasant chatty session conducted predominantly in English. A few may have perfectly accurate expectations. Thus, along with mixed motivations, the students will have mixed expectations. They may also have to be induced to 'unlearn' bad habits acquired in earlier language learning, or inaccurate and badly-pronounced language picked up somewhere else. From their schooldays they may have ideas of teacher remoteness, of formal teaching, with the students as passive learners, and with the teacher pouring in information to fill the empty spaces in their mind. In language classes they may not expect to have to talk very much, especially to each other. Teachers should therefore appreciate the need to discuss with students, before their course starts, the kind of method they hope to use, and what evidence there is of its success, for adults are much more able than children to indulge with their teacher in purposeful dialogue about the lesson. Thus, the teacher can profitably discuss with his or her class the direction in which they wish their learning to go, progress made so far, methods found enjoyable and successful. Whilst this does not necessarily imply compromising sincerely held principles on methodology, for instance, it does presuppose that a learning venture in which all participants feel personally involved, and where their ambitions and views are respected, will be more satisfying and successful than one in which they feel they have little choice and little say in what happens to them.

6) Just as their motives and expectations are mixed, adult students also come to classes with a mixture of attitudes. Rogers (7) describes these well. High in importance among these attitudes in many students is anxiety, a worry that they may not be able to cope. Coupled with this is a fear of looking foolish when making a mistake, or when experiencing difficulty. Anxieties of this kind

appear to be greater in adults than children. In some respects, mild anxiety can be an incentive to learning, which will be seen as a way of relieving the anxiety. Teachers can benefit from this, by keeping the class gently alert, and by remaining calm themselves. Alertness must not be allowed to become extreme tension, however, for this will preclude learning. 'I began to dread going - when he picked on me I nearly died.' (Quoted by Sidwell (3).)

Despite their greater age, experience, and sophistication, adults may be more reluctant than children to commit themselves in speech. They may have doubts about their capacity to learn. Consequently, they may be anxious about losing face or looking silly if they make a mistake in speech. (This may be one of the reasons why some return time and time again to a beginners' class where they feel comfortable.) Unlike other subjects in the adult curriculum, foreign language learning has two rather uncomfortable features. If the lesson is conducted exclusively in the foreign language (as no doubt, as far as possible, it should be) students often find themselves temporarily deprived of the ability to say what they want, which, after all, is the chief way in which personality can be exhibited. And in a lesson where speech is all important, mistakes will be very public. This can also cause anxieties, and consequent unwillingness to speak.

Linked to anxiety is clearly a concern about the self-image. The self-image is a very important factor in self-confidence and self-respect. It is stronger in some people than others, but even in those in whom it is strong, the recognition which comes from joining a class that there are certain areas in which they are ignorant or deficient, can threaten the self-image. It is important that the learning process should not heighten the threat.

Teachers can help to foster the self-image by praise for success in learning, and by recognition wherever possible of existing knowledge and experience. Rogers points out that a good way of doing this is by judicious use of phrases like: 'Do you remember that very good point which John made...?' Adults, like children, are sensitive to criticism, and teachers have to find ways to encourage learning and develop the self-image of the students which will necessarily involve correction, but not distress the student; in a good class, students will be mutually supportive, which will help to overcome the problem.

7) Adults bring with them, as a result of their lifetime's experience, a private knowledge, often extensive in certain areas, which may be of interest and value for the teacher and the class. For instance, I was involved with one French beginners' class which contained a young man who had travelled widely in France selling elastic, and another older man who had covered most of France in various holidays by motor-cycle, and had become very knowledgeable

on Gothic churches. Such students can be a valuable resource, and can also have their self-image reinforced if the teacher allows them to make use of their knowledge. Also as a result of increased years, adults will be more sophisicated than children in their interests, and may not respond well to what they see as childish content (cats on chairs, boys being chased by bulls). They may have a fairly rapid recognition of what is likely to be of use to them. They may also have developed sophisticated, or idiosyncratic, learning strategies, which allow them to acquire new material quite fast. This will be important, as it will allow many of them to make much more rapid progress than children do at school. The problem for the teacher will be that he or she will have to learn to cope with several different learning strategies in the group. This will affect his or her class organisation and presentation of material - something, of course, which all good teachers pay attention to.

8) Adults often arrive in class after a day's work, perhaps tired and hungry. The teacher will certainly need to devise ways of bringing them rapidly into the foreign language orbit, and to be attentive to their attitudes during the lessons. A slumped student may also have allowed his mind to slump. Although this is equally true of children in school, if an adult learner leaves the lesson in this slumped state, disenchanted or bored, he may become a statistic in the dropout rate the next week.

MEETING STUDENTS' NEEDS

Later chapters in this volume will consider in detail the more specifically methodical aspects of teaching adults. A number of points spring into prominence, however, from the discussions which have preceded.

1) Dropout is a factor to be borne in the forefront of the mind. In a very small sample of language classes taken at random, Gwen Speak- man found a very high dropout rate and came to this conclusion after interviewing the students who had abandoned the course:

'The most frequent remark was, 'It was not really what I expected', in one respect or another, and I am convinced this is largely the key to the dropout problem. For years, people have been enrolling for classes about which they know nothing beyond a title such as 'German for beginners' or 'Conversational French'. In the whole sur- vey, only sixteen people had ever spoken to the teacher before en- rolling. Eleven of these stayed throughout the course, and the other five were among those who gave purely practical reasons for leaving. Of the remaining people, seventeen stayed on. They found the course satisfactory, but as many others did not. These people feel cheated; they have wasted valuable time and money, and, more seriously, some have lost a great deal of confidence and self- esteem' (9).

The implications of this would seem to be as follows:

- Published descriptions of courses proposed should be honest, and adequately describe the aims. No false claims should be made. Language learning probably requires harder mental exertion than most other of the cluster of practically oriented subjects along with which foreign languages are grouped to form the major part of the adult curriculum provision. It is foolish, therefore, to pretend that the process is easy, or that excessively optimistic aims can be met, especially in the short time usually available. (See Chapter 5.)

- Students should be given the chance to discuss the course with the tutor, preferably in advance, e.g. at the time of enrolment. This will allow them to measure their own ambitions and expectations against the content and methodology of the course which the tutor intends to organise. It will not prevent the tutor adapting his or her ideas to some extent to accommodate the expressions of interest from potential students, but it will help prevent the indiscriminate enrolment of just any student who, for whatever reason, wishs to join a class. Positive screening and counselling will be a help to teachers, and students also are entitled to the clearest possible description of the content and organisation of courses before they pay their fee; and if subsequently they feel that they have been inadequately informed (or simply that they have misjudged), to a refund of at least part of their money, or transfer to a more appropriate class, if one is available.

- Students need to know that the teacher feels involved with them. Thus, it is a positive sign if the teacher asks for prior warning of absence whenever possible; it suggests an interest and an importance attached both to the individual and to the group. If a student fails to attend, a telephone call or friendly letter to enquire about illness or other impediment may be welcomed. It may also help to overcome the feeling that an absence will make it impossible for the student to catch up again. Finally, if numbers show signs of dropping, a discussion with the group will help students to feel that the corporate venture matters; it might also suggest reasons for some modification of approach.

- Given the nature of adults, styles of leadership are important. Adults behave differently under different types of leadership - observations of reactions to national leaders in various countries show this. In the educational context, adults certainly prefer a democratic type of organisation. In a democratically organised group, students are involved in discussions about their learning, and tend to regard the teacher more as a counsellor than a demagogue. Creativity seems to flourish more in such groups, and this may be the result of more pleasant social relationships. Among other things, groups in which students frequently talk to each other are

9

likely to have fewer problems of interpersonal relationships. Furthermore, 'the main criterion of success in such a group is that a student will feel able by the end of the course to go on learning on his own - that he has become a person capable of planning and extending his own learning' (Rogers (7)). Among other things, it is also important that the teacher be sensitive to student's reactions: Do they want to talk more? Do they want homework? Do they feel they are making progress? What do they feel about the methods employed? (This point is further developed in Chapter 4.)

2) The shortness of time available is perhaps the most important single factor in teaching languages to adults; it necessitates realism in the statement of aims. It also necessitates a teaching system which will allow those aims to be attained. This underlines the importance of attempting to form classes with broadly common ambitions and expectations.

I suggested earlier that the fact that foreign languages were grouped in that cluster of practically oriented subjects said something about the ambitions and motivation of students who enrol for language courses. For most of them want a foreign language course which is practically oriented, too. As most of them set out intending just to follow a one-year course, the biggest demand is likely to be much less for a comprehensive course which lays the foundation for a grammatically complete programme (for which several years study will be needed) than for courses which will supply the communicational needs of a relatively intelligent and independent traveller. What those needs are in detail will be discussed by other contributors to this volume, but a few points should be made at this stage.

It has been estimated (Rivers, quoted by Sidwell (10)) that in language use we spend:

45% of our time listening
30% of our time talking
16% of our time reading
9% of our time writing

Clearly, therefore, communicational needs are predominantly concerned with the ability to understand speech, and the ability to reply to it and to initiate it. The discriminating traveller will thus need - and will be quite aware of his need for - the kind of language which he or she will use in a real life interpersonal context.

As, in order to acquire it, the students will need to practise it intensively, they will clearly need the kind of language which they can use themselves, meaningfully and regularly, to their neighbours in the class. They will therefore need both the kind of organisation of learning and the kind of class organisation that will allow a good deal of inter-student communication.

3) As far as class organisation is concerned, it is clear that the students will need to be seated in such a way that they can all see each other easily, that they can work in pairs or small groups easily, and that they can circulate in the room in order to practise their newly acquired language with different partners (there being a limit to the satisfaction which can be obtained from asking the same question several times of the same neighbour). This means that the physical layout of the teaching room is important. The traditional layout of rows one behind the other will not be satisfactory - apart from anything else, almost the only eye contact possible will be between students and the teacher. If furniture can be moved, experimentation with other layouts will suggest more socially acceptable arrangements (e.g. horseshoes, hollow squares, circles, semicircles, rows facing each other), which will also facilitate work in class. 'Neither the tutor's desk nor the language lab console can be the main focus of natural, socialising conversation... let the students get to their feet... and walk around to practise the phrases to be learnt on the persons of their choice... If in the first few weeks the socialising possibilities of the language can be kept in the foreground, all our worries about how much grammar will soon drop into place' (Hay (8)). We might also find that fewer students turn their backs and walk permanently away from the class.

Classes may have a wide age range. Age does have its effects on physical and intellectual powers - not always negatively, as we have seen. At the physical level, hearing and vision decline, at differing rates. It is important for teachers to be aware of this and to ensure at least these simple things: that the room is well lit, that blackboard work is clear and uncluttered (an overhead projector may turn out to be more visible); that anyone with relatively weak vision is encouraged to sit near to the blackboard or fairly close to the screen; that speech is clear, whether from the teacher, from a tape recorder or from other students; that seating arrangements allow all students to see the teacher's face, and lip movements.

4) The organisation of learning depends very much on the teacher's syllabus and teaching procedures. Time is so short that, for instance, every minute spent speaking English potentially takes away a very important minute which could be spent speaking the foreign language. Furthermore, teacher selection of material must exclude as much material as possible which will not directly serve a communicative purpose. Students need to spend all their time listening to and speaking the foreign language in potentially useful contexts. But they need more than this. They need help in the organisation of learning which can go on outside the classroom. The traditional week's gap between lessons means that unless students are kept in touch with foreign languages in some way, they may need to spend so much time revising in the next class session that progress is dreadfully slow.

11

Students need encouragement from the beginning to realise that they must do their own learning, and that it must carry on outside the class. The willingness to do some form of homework will make a major difference to speed of acquisition of the new language. Organising oneself to do homework vigorously, maybe to listen to a tape, perhaps to do some reading (of a document prepared by the teacher, then of printed materials, and perhaps even a dictionary or a course book), and to learn not only the words which occurred in the class session but which have been met elsewhere independently – such self-organisation is difficult. Its desirability is one of the items which can benefit from adults' maturity and from their ability to discuss sensibly with the teacher what is required for their own learning.

This point is very important. The students' main need is interpersonal use of the language in lesson time. Ideally, the teacher will encourage them to do outside lesson time all of those things which they can profitably do on their own. This is one way in which the teacher can cope with differential knowledge in groups including faux-débutants, and differential aptitude and ambition between students. It is also a way in which students can move towards greater autonomy in the use of the foreign language. Such autonomy is the final objective of the language learning process for all learners; what all teachers should be aiming for is pupils who, in contact with native speakers, can manage without their teacher (11). Autonomy in this sense comes from the student building up a personal language stock, based on and working round what the tutor has taught in class, but allowing him or her to express feelings, deriving from thought patterns, social habits and interests which are personal and individual. As an example, the teacher may have taught a unit based on booking into a hotel, including the necessary types of negotiating language, what is needed to ask for services and costs, and perhaps to complain or express pleasure and appreciation. The language necessary to ask about meals and other facilities, including places of interest nearby will have been included. This material will have been extensively practised orally in class, until the majority of students seem to be able to cope confidently with it. The tutor will also have prepared a handout to distribute at the end of the lesson which contains the material taught, so that students can rehearse it during the gap before the next lesson, and which might also contain an extension of material taught, in the form of homework. However, when thinking about staying in a hotel abroad, the student knows what his or her own interests are (stamp collecting, architecture, walking, viticulture, or whatever), and by judicious use of dictionaries or other reference books will be able to build up a stock of items which may interest nobody but him or her in the class. Such research may also encourage the reading of books (perhaps in English) about things which occur to him or her as a result of the course.

Realising this, the imaginative tutor will leave time in each lesson for students to ask privately for verification of their acquisitions and will be able to provide answers both to enquiries on relevant topics, and queries of a more simply grammatical kind resulting from previous teaching. Michael Hay (8) has an example of a detailed work scheme showing how such an arrangement can be made. In this way, all students will have the chance to build up, as they must, as everybody has done in learning a foreign language, their <u>class core language</u> (what everyone has learnt), their <u>personal active language</u> (which they have acquired for themselves), and a <u>passive recognition language</u> which will be part common and part personal. Nothing increases motivation like the student's own recognition of successful progress in a topic of interest, acquiring material the practical utility of which is clear. Uniform speed and uniform progress should not be looked for in an adult class. The non-uniform nature of the student intake will preclude it, in any case.

5) There is often a decline in short term memory with age. Things learnt recently tend to be more easily displaced from the memory by new material. Thus, the learning of sequences of short new items to be memorised becomes increasingly difficult, as each new item interferes with those previously learnt. This highlights the need for language teachers to avoid approaches relying on memorisation (e.g of word lists), and to develop approaches which constantly recycle material already learnt, and which rely on acquisition and practice of complete patterns rather than of dissected pieces of grammar. Language learning requires plenty of student activity. It is important to avoid the need to 'unlearn', as this is correspondingly more difficult. This precludes the 'temporary' acceptance (which is often fairly long term), by the teacher of unacceptable forms of language use, which will be corrected in later sessions. Adults need to get things right first time and shortage of time requires this too.

Although autonomy in language use requires the opportunity to pursue open-ended questions, where answers are not totally predictable to the teacher, the early learning process should be such that the fewest errors are made, commensurate with the need to encourage students to be more adventurous later with the newly acquired language. Perhaps as much as children, adults also need the reinforcement that comes from being praised for their early success.

The teaching, especially of grammar, needs to be of the kind which, whilst giving plenty of contextualised practice of patterns, also allows the student to see the pattern clearly. Many adults have a memory which benefits from being able to work from organised constructs, preferably constructs which the student has formulated clearly for his or herself with checking from the teacher. This suggests that it may be a good idea for a portion of the lesson to be set aside for students to compose grammar notes for themselves, with the teacher on hand to verify and help. This is an approach which

13

implicitly stresses the autonomy of the learner (again the type of time organisation suggested by Hay (8) would allow for this).

6) It should not be assumed that the standard pattern of one weekly 90-minute class is the only possible organisational pattern. Some students are eager to make rapid progress, and some have been disappointed by the comparatively slow rate of progress in short weekly sessions. There is almost certainly a clientele in most areas for more intensive classes. Two sessions per week is not uncommon. In Leicestershire, we have run successful classes which met three and in one case four nights per week. Usually, classes on three or four nights per week need to be spaced over a relatively small number of weeks - perhaps just over one term, so as not to set an impossible target for students. They will almost certainly require two teachers to share the load, and these teachers will need to liaise carefully to ensure that the rapid progress promised can be maintained. It is also likely that the bulk of those students who usually enrol for a once weekly session will not enrol for one which involves four meetings a week. But our intensive classes of this kind have enrolled good class numbers, and have kept their students very successfully (with very low dropout rates indeed). This indicates that there is an audience which prefers this type of class, and which feels the need for rapid progress. In centres even of moderate population, it should be possible to satisfy such needs. By the same token, it should not be assumed that all students want the same kind of class. There may be a significant number who are at least as interested in the literature, political life, and cultural aspects of the country as in its language. It can be a nuisance for the teacher if a class intending to concentrate on language learning contains too many of these students, for he will find it difficult to satisfy all their needs and interests. Tutors should also consider organising, therefore, what might be categorised as 'land, life and language classes', which would provide opportunities for students to see films, read short stories (perhaps in translation), discuss food, see slides of the regions, investigate folklore and traditions, and perhaps learn something of the language. Such classes would need to be clearly publicised as such, in order to attract the right audience. Too much emphasis on items of the above kind in a class supposed to be for language learning can cause frustration in the students. One man who dropped out from a class said in explanation: 'The teacher was always talking about cooking and French fashions. This is not very interesting for a man.'

In whatever type of class, then, students need to recognise that the material they are learning is relevant to their needs, and both related to real life and realistic in its demands. Pronunciation of the language slowed down to a level not acceptable to native speakers will not be helpful in a real social context. Too much learning about imagined events and people, or too little language acquisition, may frustrate.

Adults will not refuse to try to work hard to acquire something they see as worthwhile, provided it is within their reach. Older people may be more considered and more methodical in their decision-making, but not necessarily slower, than younger class members. In brief, 'adults learn best when they do not have to rely on memorising, but can learn through activity at their own pace with material that seems relevant to their daily lives, and uses their own experience' (Rogers (7)). An organisation which allows of this is perhaps the best key to teaching success.

REFERENCES

(1) Department of Education and Science: Adult education, a plan for development. (The Russell Report.) HMSO, 1973, pp 226-284.

(2) Harding, C L M: Modern language study in further education. Unpublished M Ed thesis, University of Manchester, 1969. Quoted in D G Smith, D M Sidwell and R Payne: Modern language teaching. (Teaching Adults, New Series.) NIAE, October 1977.

(3) Sidwell, D M: 'A survey of modern language classes.' Adult Education,vol 52, no. 5, January 1980.

(4) Roberts, G L and W Webb: 'Factors affecting dropout.' Adult Education, vol 53, no. 2, July 1980.

(5) National Institute for Adult Education: Adult education - adequacy of provision. NIAE, 1970.

(6) Baer, E (ed): Teaching languages: ideas and guidance for teachers working with adults. BBC Publications, 1976.

(7) Rogers, J: Adults learning. Open University Press, 1977.

(8) Hay, M: Languages for adults. Longman, 1973.

(9) Speakman, G, in an unpublished thesis, Leicestershire Education Committee, n.d.

(10) Sidwell, D M, D G Smith and R Payne: Modern language teaching. (Teaching Adults, New Series.) NIAE, February 1978.

(11) Holec, H: Autonomy and foreign language learning. Council of Europe, 1979. Pergamon Press, 1981.

LANGUAGE LEARNING THEORIES AND THEIR IMPLICATIONS FOR THE CLASSROOM

Shelagh Rixon

Even teachers who claim to be exclusively practical in their approach and who question the relevance to the classroom of what theoreticians have to say are working from underlying theories of their own. Every teacher, if asked, could give an account of what students may be expected to do in a foreign language in order to say that they 'know' it in some sense. It is unlikely that what the teacher does to help students learn, or what he or she is pleased or dismayed at in the students' language performance will run counter to these underlying theories whose sources the teacher may or may not be able to trace.

It would appear that language teachers reach their personal working theories as a result of two main sets of influences:

(1) Their own experiences as language learners.

At one extreme this can result in a carbon copy of the attitudes and approaches to language learning exhibited by their own teachers with the use of exercise types that were familiar to them as learners. At the other extreme, teachers whose own experience as learners was perhaps not as successful or happy as it might have been, react by trying to provide their pupils with a very different style of teaching from that which they themselves suffered. Between the two extremes there are many degrees of conformity to or reaction against past teachers' ideals, but it would be hard to deny the influence that each generation of teachers has on the attitudes and methods of the next.

(2) Ideas current within the profession deriving from the work of applied linguists and methodology specialists.

Even if teachers themselves do not have access to the original research of the theoreticians, the results of that research tend to percolate down through the filter of in- and pre-service teacher training and through conference and staffroom discussion. Very often, especially in countries remote from the site of the research, an approach or an idea becomes part of the fashionable orthodoxy before teachers have had a chance to evaluate its usefulness or even, sometimes, to appreciate exactly what it is saying. The result can be unfortunate: possible resentment amongst those upon whom the ideas have rushed with insufficient groundwork, bandwaggonism amongst some, and embarrassment amongst others who would have liked to investigate the ideas more deeply, but for whom it is now too late to admit that they are not perfectly in command of all the details. The most recent case is that of the so-called communicative approach, which in many instances has not been sufficiently understood to be given an undistorted trial, since the equation 'communicative = good' has been arrived at before the majority of teachers have been able to inform themselves sufficiently.

Problems also arise when an idea which a teacher has accepted at a rational level, either runs counter to what he or she unconsciously feels language learning is all about or has not been fully integrated with earlier experiences. This can result in collecting together an unanalysed ragbag of classroom techniques without considering carefully enough the purposes that each one could serve in the learning process. Techniques that are quite inappropriate to stated objectives may be used without the realisation that there may be fundamental contradictions in the methodology. For example, a teacher who sees him or herself as promoting spontaneous communication in the foreign language through the use of role-play may in fact be frustrating spontaneity by making the students write out their parts beforehand and learn them off by heart.

Because the main theories of language learning which have been current during this century have probably had a direct or an indirect influence on most language teachers — through either their own or their original teachers' professional grounding or through the course books they use — it is therefore not merely a matter of historical curiosity to look at some of them in more detail. A close look at how theory has influenced classroom techniques could also throw light on the links between particular exercise-types and the teaching purposes they were meant to achieve. This may lead us to reconsider some techniques and exercises which have fallen out of favour, but which might in fact still be useful for certain purposes.

This survey falls into two main sections, the first covering some approaches current before the early 1970's and the second examining developments after this time. Although ideas derived from particular researches or theories have very rarely been carried directly into the classroom in their 'pure' state, the earlier period saw much more clear-cut links between methodologies and their underlying assumptions. Recent times have been marked by a great richness of theories about language learning which, for the most part, have complemented one another rather than competed. These have not resulted in rigid methods so much as in broad approaches managing to include many of the techniques developed in earlier times.

17

FROM THE END OF THE NINETEENTH CENTURY TO THE EARLY 1970's: GRAMMAR TRANSLATION, DIRECT METHOD, AUDIO-LINGUAL METHOD

Each methodology was clear about the models of learning they based themselves on, about what the student was supposed to be able to do with the foreign language, and about the resulting recommendations for classroom practice.

(1) GRAMMAR TRANSLATION METHOD

The teaching of modern languages by the grammar translation method derived from the same assumptions as were applied to the learning of Latin and Greek. Classical languages were seen as providing mental training as well as access to great literature and philosophy, and when modern languages were introduced to the schools during the nineteenth century the same arguments were brought forward to justify their place in the curriculum. The obvious difference between, say Latin and French – that, whereas there are no Romans left to converse with, there are many millions of French people – did not lead at first to a difference in the objectives for learning the two languages. The written form of the language was the one concentrated upon, and a successful language learner was someone who could demonstrate an ability to handle the grammar and syntax by means of translation into and out of the target language. Exercises were often performed on a series of unconnected sentences which were chosen or constructed with an eye to demonstrating a particular grammatical rule rather than to their practical usefulness. It was not, however, enough for pupils to show their knowledge in practical grammar and translation exercises. They had also to be able to talk about the language – to quote the rules and to name the parts of speech using the accepted terminology. This terminology came directly from that used for the classical languages and was not necessarily suitable for describing or categorising other languages. The use of the term 'subjunctive' for certain uses of the past form of the verb in English (as in 'If I ate that I would be sick') is an example of how the use of these terms introduced needless complications. In this method the terms in which the pupil displayed his or her knowledge were as abstract and as theoretical as those used by the teacher. This is in sharp contrast with later methods in which the pupil would be judged by his or her performance in the language rather than by knowledge of its parts. Exercises in which the student is asked, e.g. 'Write out the past perfect tense of mangiare.' 'What is the plural of il muro?' reflect this view even today, although it is clear that, used along with other techniques which allow the pupil to use the language, they may be useful in ensuring that there is an adequate grasp of grammar.

Students who succeeded in this tradition of teaching could emerge with a knowledge of the grammatical structure of a language which might form a useful basis for learning to use it after some real-life contact with native speakers. However, what they often came away with was a very limited capacity which was the result of a methodology based on the teaching of dead languages. Apart from being quite inexperienced in speaking the language or understanding it when it was spoken, the student would be hampered by his lack of contact with the normal colloquial forms of everyday language. Knowledge of the language of great literature is a worthwhile end in itself perhaps, but it does not equip one for the market place.

(2) DIRECT METHOD

The new sort of 'client' for language learning which emerged during the second half of the nineteenth century was in fact more concerned with the market place, and reinforced the move towards a methodology which would produce rapid practical command of a language rather than academic knowledge about it. Increased trade and contact between nations meant that entrepreneurs and business people began to feel the need to speak to their opposite numbers and to have a working knowledge of the languages of the countries they dealt with. Apart from the fact that they would not tolerate learning aspects of a language that seemed to them irrelevant, many of the 'new people' had not been to schools which had put them through the classical mill, and they therefore would be quite unfamiliar with the highly abstract terminology and categories through which the grammar translation method operated. The new method replaced grammatical rules where possible by a number of practical examples of a rule in operation, and presented the foreign language in a way which relied very little, if at all, on the use of the mother tongue in class. Use of pictures, mime, demonstration, induction from examples were the ways in which meaning was clarified, and when students were to speak or write, the stimulus would be a picture, an action or something said or written in the foreign language. Translation was virtually outlawed, even when it might have been useful, for example for making the meaning of a single word quickly clear. The theoretical basis for this was an analogy with the way a child learns its mother tongue: through prolonged exposure to the spoken word, through imitation, and through use of the language in a social context. Because of its basic philosophy of direct contact with and direct use of the foreign language, the term <u>direct method</u> was applied to many variants of the approach, from its most rigorous application in institutions, such as the Berlitz schools, to the methods discussed by Palmer in the 1920's and '30's (1).

Most of the class work was oral, with great importance given to accurate acceptable pronunciation and the ability to understand the spoken language when produced naturally and at normal speeds. The developments in the study of phonetics from the end of the nineteenth century onwards gave course designers and teachers more information about how sounds were produced and reinforced the preference for spoken practice in class. In fact, many direct method practitioners saw the use of reading and writing, at least in the early stages of learning, as a source of interference with correct pronunciation and as a hindrance to learning through the spoken word.

Although it had its roots in the need to give adult students a practical grasp of foreign languages, the direct method soon became influential in schools, reaching its peak around the '20's and '30's of this century. In some cases schools introduced features which adult clients probably would not have tolerated, such as the teaching of phonetic symbols to children in the hope of helping their pronunciation. This rather abstract approach to the problem is an echo perhaps of the idea seen already in grammar translation teaching, that the pupil's knowledge should be of the same kind as the teacher's. It would have been quite possible for the teachers to use their knowledge of phonetics to aid students' speech without imposing phonetics as a subject in itself upon their classes.

The main contribution of the direct method to methodological development was in the heavy exposure it gave learners to the foreign language, and in the active practice they were given right from the beginning. In the best teaching there was also some common-sense progression in the complexity of the language introduced, but there was as yet no systematic framework available for the choice and ordering of items to be taught within a course. The grammatical categories used by the grammar translation method did not offer a solution since they merely presented whole paradigms, e.g. the whole of the present tense of the 'model verb' to be learned in one go. The idea of graded difficulty had yet to be developed fully.

(3) STRUCTURALISM AND AUDIO-LINGUAL METHODOLOGY

This need for the language content of courses to be more systematically organised was met in the late '30's and '40's as a result of applying the techniques used by structural linguistics to describe exotic languages, to languages such as English or French. Broadly, the relevant techniques involve taking any grammatical string of words in a language and investigating how it can be segmented into parts where substitutions may be made. For example, in the French sentence Elle mange du pain the word mange consists of two elements, the root mang- and the ending. Other endings must be substituted if the pronoun is changed, e.g. Vous mang-ez du pain. Equally, whole words may be substituted, provided that they fit the permitted grammatical 'slot' for that language, e.g. Nous trouvons du pain, Nous trouvons du beurre, Il trouve du beurre, Pierre trouve du beurre, etc. The use of such techniques served a double purpose. Firstly, the sentences of the foreign language could be broken down into their component parts and put into a logical order so that as far as possible new learning was built upon items that had already been covered. For example, in the sentences above we could assume

20

that the du pain element had already figured in earlier lessons involving the je and il forms of the same verbs, with the sentence about Pierre reintroduced as revision. This learning by small systematic steps is very characteristic of structuralist-influenced teaching. The second consequence of this influence is the substitution table, a device still used even in courses which would proclaim themselves as based on very different principles. To use the examples of the French sentences once more and observing where the lines of segmentation could come, a table such as that below can be constructed.

je il elle	mange	du	pain beurre
tu	manges	de la	viande confiture
nous	mangeons		
vous	mangez		
ils elles	mangent		

Following the simple rule that items separated by a horizontal line may not be substituted one for the other, but items arranged one under the other in the same 'box' can be substituted, a learner reading across the table is guaranteed always to form a grammatically correct sentence. So far what we have is a useful modification of the direct method in terms of the way in which language is presented, but other factors combined to produce an approach that became quite distinct and gained the label of audio-lingualism.

The first factor is linked with the possibility of being able to grade the content of a language course and so to arrange the exercises through the use of substitution tables and similar graphic displays that the students need never, in theory, make mistakes. The behavioural psychologist B F Skinner (2) was at this time working on a theory which saw learning as the result of the reinforcement by reward or other gratification of a particular piece of behaviour. By selectively rewarding behaviour in an animal, such as a rat or a pigeon, he was able to train the animal to perform a specific action if given a specific stimulus. So, for example, he could train a pigeon to peck at a circle every time a green light went on. To achieve this he would let the pigeon peck at random and then every time it happened to peck at the circle while the light was on it would get a reward. The pigeon would only get a reward if it pecked at the circle while the light was on. In the end the pigeon would be

21

conditioned to peck at the circle because the light came on - it would associate the stimulus of the light with the response of pecking even without reward every time the stimulus of the light was given. In this way Skinner trained or 'shaped' behaviour. This behaviourist learning theory became applied to language learning at a time when all the facilities for its application were there. Structural linguistics had provided the means of breaking down languages into small, logically ordered, learning steps. The development of sound recording, and of the tape recorder in particular allowed teachers to present their students with an accurate and tireless model of the language. The development of the substitution table and exercises in which the student repeated sentences making small changes to the substitutable elements each time combined with these to provide a role for language drills with the tape recorder and eventually with the language laboratory. If the job of the language teacher was now seen as one of shaping a pupil's linguistic behaviour by the provision of stimulus (drill sentences for correct repetition, substitution or transformation, e.g. singular to plural) and reward in the form of approval for a correct response, the language laboratory with its provision for simultaneous practice for all the class and a tireless and accurate repetition from the tapes was seen as his or her most effective tool. Because learning was seen as coming about through repetition, the greatest pains were taken to avoid mistakes on the part of the students in case they should 'learn their mistakes' and become saddled with wrong linguistic habits. The learning tasks were broken down into such very small steps in the attempt to avoid error that often students complained of boredom and of the lack of challenge. Because the practice sentences were chosen to enable the student to practise elements of the grammatical structure of the language, they also suffered from the same sort of disease that the grammar translation examples exhibited: an insufficient concern with commonsense meaning. The audio-lingual equivalent of 'the pen of my aunt...' is the type of drill in which the student is led to utter grammatically correct but mutually contradictory sentences, such as 'I like ice cream. I don't like ice cream' just for the sake of practising the different forms.

Quite apart from this aspect of meaning, dissatisfaction with audio-lingual methodology was expressed when it came to language as part of the expression of social meaning. The concern of audio-lingual teaching is essentially inward-looking, concentrating on contrasts within the language system itself, and typified by pronunciation and sound discrimination exercises concentrating on minimal distinctions, such as that between 'beach' and 'peach', which would be unlikely to cause confusion in the context of a whole sentence, let alone in real life. It was noticed again and again that students who performed well in the confines of the classroom lacked flexibility and were at a loss when they found themselves in real life having to use the language. So-called situational courses were usually a variant on audio-lingual teaching. They attempted to make more of a connection between grammar practice and real life by setting each lesson in an everyday scene, e.g. 'at the post office', 'in the park', and working largely through dialogues illustrating the target language. However, the needs of the grammatical syllabus still tended to dominate so that the dialogues and drills resulting from these scenes were more likely to consist of a set of prescribed structures forced into dramatic framework than an accurate reflection of what would actually be said in such situations. Sometimes a situational unit might even consist of a third-person description of a transaction in, for example, a post office. This would convey even less useful information about language in social use than an artificial dialogue.

THEORY AND APPROACHES IN TEACHING SINCE THE EARLY SEVENTIES

THE COMMUNICATIVE APPROACH

It is from the early 1970's onwards that the view of language as something that operates within society has been gaining ground as the subject of theoretical study. This has had a major influence on the redefinition of the objectives of language study and on decisions about the appropriate content and methodology for language courses. Teachers who have been influenced by this more sociological view of language may use differing classroom techniques, but their objective is the same: to enable students to communicate effectively with other people who use the foreign language. Effectiveness includes the concept of social appropriateness or acceptability - of using language to get along with people - as well as that of grammatical accuracy which was the more limited aim of audio-lingualism.

The label 'communicative' probably derives from Dell Hyme's work on communicative competence. This was principally concerned with the native speaker's ability in his or her own language and extended our view of competence in a language beyond grammar alone and into areas where language is a part of social behaviour. It is these areas in which the language learner is often under-informed, if at all, and in which the greatest pitfalls lie. One can, for example, know Italian grammar perfectly, but be unskilled in judging when to use the formal or the intimate form of 'you'. One may speak good German but not know the words that a real German would use to invite guests to help themselves at table. A classic set of examples by Newmark shows the attempts of someone who speaks grammatical English, but does not know the formula to get a light from a stranger 'Have you fire?' 'Are you a matches owner?' etc.

These last examples concern formulae which are part of the native speaker's competence but not necessarily part of the learner's, but it is the area of language appropriate to differing social situations which provides the greatest challenge to teacher and learner alike. 'Situation' here includes the speaker's relationship with the people he or she is with, the purpose for which he or she is communicating, the channel (spoken, written) they are using for communication, 'outside' circumstances such as noise, emergency, etc. Once language teachers begin to take seriously the fact that competent speakers vary in the ways in which they express the same meanings according to the situation, the complexity of the learner's task is understood, particularly in view of the fact that research into what actually happens among native speakers is at such an early stage. The risk of forming stereotypes of what happens in, say, a formal business meeting in France is high, but there is a gain in that we have at least realised the problem.

Students often came out of an audio-lingual course with the false impression that there was a one-to-one correspondence between a grammatical form and a particular meaning. For example, they might think that the way to ask people to do things in English is to use the imperative, softened a little where particular politeness is required by the use of 'please'. The fact is that a request in the form 'Open the window, please' would tend to give offence as too brusque and direct in all but the most close of social relation-ships or situations of urgency. Dissatisfaction with this state of affairs made teachers and course designers eager to follow applied linguists in finding a new way of thinking about language in use.

Functions

The concept of language functions has been one of the most fruitful so far from the point of view of course design. A function, broadly, describes what it is that speakers or writers are trying to do through the language at a particular moment. Are they, for example, trying to warn me of something when they say 'This soup's hot' or are they complimenting me on providing something comforting on a cold day? They might even be complaining that my soup was too hot to eat! The point is that, without taking the real or imagined context into account, it is impossible to know what a particular person is actually trying to communicate through the language. An analysis of an utterance at the purely grammatical level will be of no help at all.

Conversely, one can take a single function, for example 'inviting', and think of many ways of expressing it according to the person one is addressing, and whether one is speaking or writing;
'You are cordially invited to a reception....
I'm having a party next Sunday....
Would you be free to come round next Sunday? I'm having a party....
My place next Sunday, 8 o'clock, right?'
These would all be possible ways of expressing the function of 'inviting', but the choice would depend on factors such as how well

the people knew one another, whether the invitee already knew about the party, how hurried or leisurely the conversation was, etc.

Courses which are organised on functional lines tend to have unit headings listing functions, such as the above and others, such as 'requesting', 'apologising', 'promising', in contrast to the units of a grammar translation course which might have headings, such as 'the present tense', 'first conjugation of verbs', or those of a situational course, such as 'at the bank'. Audio-lingual courses preferred to be less overt in the information they gave the student and often units were named by an extract of the language they contained, e.g. 'I'm going to...'.

One of the main aims of functional courses is to draw the students' attention to the different choices available in one language for expressing the same meaning, and to make them sensitive to the need to choose the appropriate forms for the situation they find themselves in. This aim leads to a number of difficulties. Firstly, because a range of different language forms have to be presented together in the same unit if the question of choice amongst them is to be dealt with, a functionally organised course has to sacrifice the clarity and simplicity of progression through increasingly complex grammatical structures that characterised structurally organised audio-lingual courses. This has led to criticisms such as, 'Functional courses look like old-fashioned phrase-books' or, 'They don't teach grammar in functional courses'. While both of these are exaggerations, they do point to the difficulty that teachers and course writers find in conveying both grammatical and social information at the same time. One popular solution has been to use functional courses as revision work for students who have already passed through a grammatically-oriented course. Many so-called functional courses are in fact a compromise, following a structural syllabus, but making sure that the student is well informed about the real-life uses to which the language they introduce can be put. It is thus not uncommon to see a unit in a book which covers, say, the present simple tense, but which is headed 'Giving information about things you do every day'.

Notional courses

Another possible way of organising a language course is according to the notions you want to express. In this technical sense a notion is an abstract concept, such as 'time', 'location', 'comparison', 'result'. It is easy to see how concepts such as these could be expressed by the use of a fairly limited number of grammatical categories and vocabulary items, such as the use of the past tense system and adverbs of time in the case of time, or prepositions in the case of location. In practice, far fewer courses have adopted notions as an organising principle, although some courses in English for Science and Technology have made use of notions, such as 'measurement' or 'comparison' as the subject of teaching units, and have attempted to collect together the commonest ways of expressing these concepts in scientific English.

Functions and notions in syllabus design

Functions and notions have in many ways proved far more useful as a means of providing a framework for syllabus design than they have in the writing of textbooks and courses. They provide a neat way of listing the language needs of a particular set of students. For example, in designing a syllabus for a group of scientists anxious to take part in discussions at international conferences, it is much clearer to start by listing the types of functions and notions they will need to express. They will probably need to be able to handle the functions of 'persuasion', '(polite) contradiction', 'requesting information', 'description' and so on. The notions they will need to express will include 'comparison' and 'contrast', 'measurement' and '(degrees of) probability'. Once having arrived at a list of headings such as these, the grammatical items used to express them can then be collected under each heading, to form one component of the syllabus. Vocabulary items also needed by the students can be gathered by an analysis of the topics likely to be of interest to them. Another set of information which will influence the shape of the final syllabus will be the language skills in which the students will be expected to operate, in the case of the conference-going scientist listening and speaking rather than reading and writing.

Needs analysis and course design

The above example of the use of functions and notions as part of the process of syllabus design took as its starting point the needs of a particular group of students. This is another radical change that has taken place in recent years. Earlier language teaching movements more or less assumed that every student's goal was (or should be) to learn all the foreign language. To a certain extent students' progress was measured against the Everest of the 'the French language' or 'the German language', a depressing perspective which somehow always left them conscious of their deficit rather than what they actually knew. The concept that even the 'general' student of a language, let alone someone with special purposes for learning it, like a tourist, operator or a shop assistant only needs a small and specifiable portion of the foreign language is a liberating one for the student, and one that has led to exciting projects in the design of syllabuses to suit different groups. The Council of Europe has led the way in this respect, and in ways it has expressed the syllabuses in terms of notional and functional categories.

Analysis of language skills

Closer attention to language skills is also a product of a needs-analysis approach to syllabus and course design. Previous traditions tended to think in terms of four skills – reading, writing, speaking and listening – as if they were monolithic and very separate activities instead of clusters of smaller skills. In the case of shop assistants needing French to deal with customers in a large English store it is clear that the skills of paramount importance to them will be listening and speaking. Such a bald statement is not, however, very useful to those who have to teach them. It is possible to break down the type of listening skills, for example, that they will need to cope with their job: fairly short stretches of French from customers, rather than long formal speeches, but heard against a background of distracting noises from the rest of the shop. It is unlikely that they will have to react to a very wide range of language from customers, so their task will be eased. A course in French which emphasised listening to long unpredictable monologues, upon which detailed notes were to be taken, would obviously not be appropriate to students even though it was called a 'listening course'.

Implications of needs analysis for testing and assessment

Now that reasonably precise goals for language teaching can be set, it is equally possible to devise tests which reflect those goals, and again operate in the area of what it is the student can do, rather than showing up what is not known of the language as a whole. An example of such testing can be seen in the graded objectives assessments of pupils' attainment in languages such as French and German at present being carried out in a number of areas of the United Kingdom. The result of such assessments is a description of what the pupil should be able to do in real life rather than a percentage mark of 'correct' answers. For example, a lower level certificate of this type might read 'This candidate is able to respond appropriately to everyday greetings in French, to ask for ordinary items in a shop and to react correctly to simple notices giving instructions and prohibitions'. The test itself is as far as possible a reconstruction of the type of conversations that might be expected to take place in these circumstances, held between the assessor and the candidate. More and more, the results of tests are being expressed in the form of descriptions of performance, or of levels of performance in particular skill areas. A candidate is likely to come away with a profile of his language abilities ('high on listening for information, weak on discussion skills, etc') rather than an inscrutable number or letter grade.

Methodology of the communicative approach

The survey so far has concerned factors which have shaped the communicative approach in the area of teaching objectives and course content, but new and expanded objectives create the need for new

27

methods in the classroom. This does not mean that we have to throw out well-established techniques dating from earlier approaches. Drills can still be a useful way to help students fix forms and sentence patterns in their minds, for example. However, there is clearly no point in setting out to foster flexibility and responsiveness in students if you lack the classroom techniques or the ability to create conditions which favour their development on these lines. Typically, communicative methodology revolves around activities which encourage students to take risks, in order to help them develop strategies for making the most of their small stock of language. Taking risks and experimenting with the language inevitably means making mistakes - something which audio-lingual methodology did all it could to avoid, and which the grammar translation method tended to disapprove of and to regard as carelessness on the part of the student. The teacher, in the communicative approach, must not only be willing to set up activities in which error is bound to occur as the students struggle to get their meaning across, but must be prepared to abandon the traditional rule of the 'knower' and ultimate authority who decides what it is that the students ought to know, and to act more as informant or consultant as the students find out for themselves what it is they cannot do or wish to know. This general philosophy is supported by current research on student interlanguage (the stages through which learners go on their way to command of a language), particularly that by Professor Corder of Edinburgh University (3). This suggests that those learners who are prepared to take risks and to learn from the feedback on their struggles with the language, are far more likely to develop into successful language users.

In order to make students stretch their language resources and take risks the most commonly used classroom techniques are practical tasks in which the students cooperate, giving each other information and instructions in the foreign language. For example, one student has to build a simple model following instructions from another, who has either a diagram of how to build the model or a version of the model itself held out of sight of the first student. Tasks such as this illustrate the principle of the information gap which is one of the fundamentals of communicative methodology. An information gap is set up by having one student in possession of information which another does not have, but needs in order to complete some task. This provides a motive for students to communicate with one another. It is important, of course, that the second student should not be able to get the information in any other way than through use of language, or this would destroy the motivation. If, for example, the second student could see the model or the diagram, there would be no point in the two students talking about it. (Examples of such activities are given in Chapter 4.)

Techniques such as this also provide a way for students to judge their own success. If they manage to complete an information-gap task through use of the foreign language, however many grammatical slips there may have been, they have clearly succeeded in communicating and they do not need the teacher to tell them this!

Work in pairs and small groups is integral to the communicative approach, not only because it provides each student with much more opportunity to talk, but because this kind of interaction gives students experience in reacting to their partners, in dealing with unexpected utterances, and in sorting out misunderstandings. The objectives of flexibility and increased sensitivity to others' reactions are much better met in this type of class organisation than in the rather impersonal and mechanical practice given by language laboratory work.

Other common techniques of the communicative approach involve role play, usually of a type in which students need to make a choice amongst possible expressions in order to find the most appropriate to the social situation represented in the activity. An activity without any choice, i.e one in which the students simply learned a fixed dialogue, would perhaps be providing language practice, but certainly not communicative practice.

Product and process

With communicative techniques, much of the onus is on the student. The emphasis is on the processes that one goes through - learning to improve strategies for dealing with difficulty and finding out for oneself what one needs to know in the foreign language. There is less emphasis on the product - the actual language arrived at during this process. The teacher's role in this new emphasis is more that of a collaborator than a stern drill-master and corrector of mistakes; someone who works more with the students than on them.

Such techniques do not rule out the teacher adopting a role at some times similar to that of the presenter of the new language, the leader in drill activities, or the explainer of difficulties familiar from other approaches. It is simply that the communicative approach seeks to extend the possible roles of the teacher to include one which reflects a concern with the process by which students become better users of a foreign language.

Within the communicative approach there is considerable leeway for different emphases. Some courses, for example, pay more attention to making sure that the language items they contain are useful and accurate reflections of real-life language use. Others concentrate on particular exercise types, such as role-play or problem-solving in pairs or small groups. There is far less uniformity in the methods used in classrooms which would claim to form part of the communicative movement than one might have encountered within, say, the grammar translation or audio-lingual tradition.

Throughout this survey I have tried to show how, as the focus has shifted to different aspects of language ability, changes in teaching methods have tried to produce in the students the type of ability that was thought important at the time – knowledge about as well as of a language in the grammar translation movement, practical oral command in the direct method, accuracy of grammatical structure in audio-lingualism and, finally, appropriacy and flexibility as well as accuracy in communicative approach. None of the objectives of past methods can be considered worthless in itself. Problems only arise when the wrong set of objectives is imposed on the wrong set of students, or when methods developed to meet one set of objectives are mistakenly used in the hope of meeting a completely different aim.

The most recent developments are encouraging in the sense that teaching has become more of a matter of cooperation between teacher and students. It has been seen that it is possible for them to work together on discovering real needs rather than needs imagined for them by distant authorities, and for them to work out the best ways of achieving clearly defined objectives. In some cases these means could well include techniques associated with audio-lingual, direct method, or grammar translation teaching. The concept of abstract loyalty to any particular 'method' is breaking down under the influence of more rigorous investigation into the varied objectives language learners may have and the best means of achieving each one. The 1980's may well be the period in which eclecticism in teaching methods becomes more respectable simply because it is an eclecticism informed by the results of research.

REFERENCES

(1) Palmer, Harold E: The principles of language study. Oxford University Press, 1964.

(2) Skinner, B F: Verbal behaviour. Appleton–Century–Crofts, 1957. Methuen, 1959.

(3) Corder, S Pit: Strategies of communication. Publications de l'Association Finlandaise de Linguistique Appliqué, 1977, and 'The significance of learners' errors'. International Review of Applied Linguistics, vol 5, 1967.

FURTHER READING

Chomsky, N: Review of B F Skinner 'Verbal behaviour'. In L A Jakabovits and M S Miron (eds): Readings in the psychology of language. Prentice Hall, Englewood Cliffs, NJ, 1967.

Johnson, K and K Morrow (eds): Communication in the classroom: applications and methods for a communicative approach. Longman, 1981. (Longman Handbooks for Language Teachers.)

Palmer, Harold M: The teaching of oral English. Longman, 1956. (First published 1940.)

Sweet, Henry: The practical study of languages: a guide for teachers and learners. Oxford University Press, 1964. (First published 1899.)

van Ek, J: The threshold level of modern language learning in schools. Longman, 1977.

Wilkins, D: Linguistics in language teaching. Edward Arnold, 1972.

MAIN CHARACTERISTICS OF THE METHODS DISCUSSED

	Grammar-translation	Direct	Audio-lingual	Communicative
What the student was supposed to be able to do	Translate from one language to another. Know, apply and quote the grammar rules.	Express himself or herself and understand the language.	Produce accurate fluent utterances in the language, automatically without thinking too much about grammar.	Use the language fluently as a means of interacting with other people. Getting the message over, and being socially acceptable, more important than accuracy.
Role of teacher	The authority and judge of performance.	The kindly active guide and leader of activity.	The efficient and lively drill-master.	The collaborator in students' learning.
Attitude to error	A regrettable evidence of lack of care or of ignorance.	Not a cause for concern - sufficient practice will iron it out.	Avoid it, in case students 'learn their mistakes'.	An inevitable consequence of experiment and risk taking.
Typical interaction patterns	Teacher to pupils. Pupils speak or respond only when told.	Teacher to pupils Pupils freer to participate than in grammar translation.	Teacher or mechanical device e.g tape recorder/lang lab provides stimulus to which students respond.	Students to student independently as well as teacher to students.

MAIN CHARACTERISTICS OF THE METHODS DISCUSSED (continued)

	Grammar-translation	Direct	Audio-lingual	Communicative
Typical exercise types	Translation. Application of grammar rules. Writing out grammatical paradigms.	Describing teachers actions. Responding to questions in the foreign language.	Oral drills.	Information gap problem solving. Role play.
Main skills emphasis	Reading and writing.	Listening and speaking.	Listening and speaking.	Depends on students' needs, but heavy use of oral work usually.
Underlying Theories	One learns words, grammatical forms, etc by repetition, but correct language use depends on the conscious application of a formal grammatical rule.	One learns a foreign language like a child his or her native language – by listening, repetition and use.	Language learning is a matter of forming correct habits. Error is a result of wrong habit-formation.	Language learning is more than learning grammatical structures. People learn through interaction with others, developing strategies of communication. Error is a natural part of the development of a learner towards full command of a language.

SYLLABUS DESIGN AND MULTI-MEDIA COURSE ORGANISATION

John L M Trim

The preceding chapter has demonstrated the need for the teacher of foreign languages to adults to be his own linguist, outlining some of the principal theoretical principles a teacher should understand and their main implications for teaching. All teachers need this knowledge in order to plan their work effectively and to understand what is happening in the classroom. It is not so different from what is asked of other professionals. A patient expects the doctor to understand his illness, diagnose its nature and causes and then find a proper treatment. A car-owner expects a mechanic to identify the cause of malfunction in the machine and put it right. The student/teacher relation is of course not quite the same, but here again a layman, who wants to acquire knowledge and skills in a new area, places himself in the hands of a professional expert whom he expects not only to have a thorough knowledge and well-developed skills, but to be able to communicate them, to guide the learner's development, understanding and overcoming the difficulties that arise along the way. That is as true of teachers and students in arts, crafts and sports as it is of mathematics and economics or computing and accountancy. Language teaching has, perhaps, a unique place because of the way that knowledge and skills, both mental and physical, are combined.

Listening and speaking, reading and writing are perhaps the most complex activities human beings engage in, but there is little on the surface to show for it. We come to take altogether for granted our extraordinary ability to attach meanings to tiny differences in air pressure or the direction of a pencil line, to produce long sequences of finely differentiated movements or to identify and interpret them, all without apparent effort. It is only when we start to enquire carefully into the language faculty that we begin to appreciate its complexity and richness. In spite of intensive efforts throughout this century, building on many centuries of grammatical study, linguists, psychologists and neurologists are far from a full understanding of the nature of language, the way it is acquired or learnt, or the way the brain stores linguistic knowledge and experience and manages the processes by which speech is organ- ised and produced, perceived and interpreted. Until much more is known, language teaching will remain an art rather than a science. Teachers should pay heed to what applied linguistics has to offer in the way of ideas and to the results of empirical investigations.

They should take full advantage of wider, more detailed, more systematic descriptions of languages, or aspects of languages, as they appear. They must beware of premature certainties and avoid dogmatism. They must be prepared to experiment in the light of a critical commonsense, reflect on experience and learn from it. They should keep the interests of learners paramount, learning to release and canalise their energies and remember how much depends on the development of genuine human relations. The classical characteristics of a good teaching personality – unforced authority, clarity, empathy, warmth – are as important now as ever. Much can be done to develop a teaching personality, though the spontaneity which is an important part of it resists advance planning and conscious control.

These considerations do not, of course, mean that a teacher can neglect the proper planning of courses and lessons. Indeed, one of the main reasons for careful advance planning is that it frees the teacher's mind to respond to the situations, only partly foreseeable, which arise from minute to minute in the classroom, as learners react in different ways to new material and tasks. Much of what is written here will be very familiar to experienced teachers, who may feel that it is too self-evident to deserve re-stating. Nevertheless, much of what is said and written in the field of educational technology, often because of the language used, appears to dehumanise the classroom and reduce the teacher to managerial anonymity. In my experience, that is in fact never intended, but it is a ghost that should be firmly exorcised. Explicit syllabuses and multi-media systems may appear, even in what is written in this chapter, to lead a life of their own. They do not, of course. They provide only a scaffolding, a framework to assist the interaction of teachers and students which leads to effective learning. At this point, a word of warning in the opposite direction is perhaps in order. A charismatic teacher may mount a brilliant display of class manipulation which dazzles the observer and indeed the class, which can be manipulated into a frenetic activity enjoyed by all and becoming an end in itself. But is it? If the aim of adult education is to drag people out of their television chairs to enjoy an evening working with others in a group activity, the answer is clearly 'yes'. If on the other hand students are coming to the class in order to learn the language for a purpose, the success of the course is to be judged by the extent to which they have learnt what they need to know and be able to do in order to use the language to accomplish that purpose. The activity of the teacher and even the enjoyment of the class are secondary. This note of caution is not intended to denigrate a particular style of teaching, or to say that learning should be solemn. Far from it. Learning and teaching are not just means to an end. They are part of life itself and life should be enjoyable. But unless we are to be hedonists, for whom the enjoyment of the moment is everything, we have to see learning as having a purpose, and teaching as secondary to learning.

In recent years a great deal of thought has been given to the way in which language courses should be planned. The first question which arises is: how much advance planning do we want? Opinions vary widely. At one extreme are those who think that the only way to learn a language properly is to live for a year or so in the country and pick the language up by sheer immersion in daily life. The best we can do in a classroom is then to do our best to create similar conditions and let nature take its course. At the other extreme are those who combine a Kiplingesque determination to 'fill the unforgiving minute with sixty seconds-worth of distance run' with a belief in the efficiency of the assembly line. Learners are to be processed from raw material into final products and there is no time or place for spontaneity. Most of us would be unwilling to accept either analogy. We cannot compare, say, three hours a week with sixteen hours a day and we can observe that simple immersion may lead to no more than a stunted pidgin. On the other side, an over-rigid technocratic training method which allows no freedom to teachers or students seems unlikely to help learners to become willing and able to reach out to bridge communication gaps with fellow human beings in situations which are new and largely unforeseeable. Assembly lines are best left to automata. Limited resources make it necessary to plan ahead, so that learning can be purposeful and effective, while the 'human use of human beings' makes it advisable to make the most of the informed, insightful, free interaction of students and teachers.

We should also remember that the classroom is not such an isolated place as it may sometimes seem. Behind the teacher stand many 'partners for learning' of different kinds, who can be seen as giving support to teachers and learners, or as putting them in a straitjacket. A course-book writer has already gone a long way to pre-empt the choices of teacher and learner, both as to content and, to a large extent, method. For instance, textbook writers and examiners both take some part of the responsibility for planning out of the hands of teachers and learners. That can save a lot of people a great deal of time and effort, but is bought at a cost and brings its own dangers. If new teachers are told 'We use <u>Sprich aber doch mal endlich mit, du!</u> or <u>Grammaire pratique du français contemporain</u> here. The class has got to lesson six in book two. You start on Thursday evening', do they know what they and the learners in their charge are being committed to? An inexperienced teacher may have no confidence to step outside the routine prescribed by a textbook, of reading out a prose passage or dialogue, drilling structures and vocabulary, setting the substitution and gap-filling exercises for homework, marking them with red ink according to the number of mistakes. As experience grows, the teacher may in fact become more dependent on the textbook, knowing by heart what comes next, what difficulties and errors to expect from what kind of student and a hundred tricks for getting over them. Yet mastering the textbook becomes an end in itself; the syllabus it incorporates, as well as the values and beliefs which underlie that syllabus, become unexamined presuppositions, taken uncritically for granted and hardly, if at all, entering into consciousness.

That is even more the case, perhaps, with examinations, which all too readily become the tail that wags the dog. Many teachers feel that if they are working towards an examination, their prime responsibility to their students is to get as many of them through as possible in the highest possible grades. The students are more than likely to take the same view, especially if it is put to them by the teacher. From that point on, the classroom is the setting for a conspiracy between teachers and students as to how to beat the system! If a class is working towards an examination, its syllabus sets out the objectives to be worked to. In many cases there is no syllabus worthy of the name, so that teachers and students have to work out from the papers set over a period of years what exactly it is the examiners want. That may work for content, but not for the standard expected. Only teachers with long experience of which students achieve which grades can assess the standard.

As with so many structures within which our social activity takes place, textbooks and examinations provide a supportive framework as long as they are appropriate but become straitjackets if they are not. This is already true at school, where the children are at least of the same age and with roughly the same experience and follow the same course of learning over a period of years. There already we see many strains and stresses as different types of pupil respond favourably or unfavourably to the one, monolithic course which is to be followed by everybody. In the case of adult language learning, however, the problems are greatly increased. Adults are rarely, if ever, constrained to re-enter the educational process. If they do so, they do so for what seems to them a good reason, and the reasons vary very greatly from one person to another. Some people are confronted at relatively short notice with the need to use a language in connexion with their employment. Others may wish to improve the quality of the holidays they take in the country concerned. Yet others may have family connexions by birth or marriage with whom they wish to establish communication across the language barrier.

It is not only the purposes that adults have in mind which vary widely. They come back into education at all ages, with very different educational backgrounds, study habits and expectations. They may already have studied the language for a university degree or may have no knowledge of it whatever. The establishment of separate classes at elementary, intermediate and advanced levels can go some way towards coping with differences of previous experience and the proficiency gained from that experience but can otherwise do little to meet the wide diversity of needs and learner types. Considerable frustration and a correspondingly high drop-out rate is, alas, only too often found when teachers cannot respond to the needs and demands of their pupils in an appropriate way.

In recent years, a good deal of thought has been given to ways of overcoming this problem and particularly to giving the teacher in the classroom access to syllabus planning tools which will make it possible for worthwhile and realistic objectives and methods to be negotiated with students. Of course there are limits as to how far the process of negotiation can go. Negotiation takes time and is likely to be rather unequal. When they first attend a course students often have only vague and confused ideas as to why they are learning a language and what it is that they need for their own communicative purposes. They cannot, even if they have achieved clarity in these respects, work out unaided what balance of knowledge and skills they require and can achieve within a given time under the conditions of study that are possible for them. In most cases they have no idea as to how to organise their own learning activity and usually expect, as a result of their earlier experience at school, to simply carry out the directions of the teacher. In some cases adults even regress to childhood patterns of behaviour when confronted with teachers and do not think in terms of exercising mature responsibilities which they take for granted in other parts of their life.

Under these conditions negotiation is in no way an abdication of responsibility by the teacher. Leadership is necessary to increase the self-awareness and responsibility of the adult learner. Nevertheless, it is only in this way that a heterogeneous class of adults with disparate experience and needs can be brought to see what interests they share and where they should be doing different things largely on their own initiative.

To work in this way the teacher needs to be not simply a repository of knowledge of and about the language. This personal competence is, of course, an essential prerequisite to effective teaching but by no means all that is required. To be a dynamic animator and orchestrator of classroom activity is of great importance but is perhaps not in itself sufficient. The ability to guide and organise the learning of individuals, with a substantial self-study component and work in the classroom playing an essential but limited part, is perhaps of the greatest importance. This shift in the role of the teacher _vis à vis_ the students is relatively new but seems to be, perhaps, the key to success in the special conditions of adult language teaching.

Since 1971, the Council of Europe has sponsored a series of projects in which the concepts of a 'needs-based, learner-centred language systems development' has been successively developed and refined. Essentially, the approach involves the following processes:

1) the identification of the learner's needs (especially his need to communicate), motivations and important learner characteristics, as well as the resources which are available to him or her;

2) the establishment on the basis of the above analysis of a concrete set of operational objectives which the learner must reach in order to communicate in accordance with his needs;

3) methods and materials that will bring the learner from where he is now to the achievement of his stated objectives;

4) means of assessing progress and evaluating the success of the programme for the information of all concerned.

A general account of this work is contained in Trim (1980) and in the report Modern languages 1971-1981 published by the Council of Europe. Having adopted the systems approach outlined above, the group of experts established by the Council of Europe concentrated its attention on the operational specification of language learning objectives. Since the Council of Europe is particularly concerned with the freer movement of people and ideas between its member countries, the group did not follow the earlier practice of selecting vocabulary and even grammatical structures on statistical grounds, but rather explored particularly the variety of communicative situations into which adults might enter and the kind of language activity in which they would then be involved. The resulting model specifies the following components:

1) the situations in which the language will be used. Specifying a situation means stating the roles a language learner has to play, the settings in which he will have to play them and the topics he will have to deal with; in short, the complex of extra-linguistic conditions which determines the nature and occurrence of a speech-act.

2) the language activities in which the learner will engage. These are largely conversational, but include listening to and reading public announcements and notices, and limited written communication.

3) what the learner will be able to do with respect to each topic. They should, for instance, be able to exchange information about themselves and their families, where and under what conditions they live, their school lives and future career plans, their hobbies and interests, relations with other people. They should be able to manage personal relations and transact the business of everyday life in travelling and shopping.

4) the language functions which the learner will fulfil. These include not only volunteering information, but asking and answering questions, making offers and accepting or declining them, greeting, thanking, promising, apologizing, agreeing, disagreeing, expressing approval, disapproval, love, hate and indifference, etc.

5) the general notions which the learner will be able to handle. These relate to the general framework of ideas the learner needs to express which are not tied to a particular situation, but are

generalised from experience – the categories of entities and events, their existential, essential and accidental properties and the quantitative and qualitative relations between them; the concepts of space and time, causality and other logical relations.

6) the specific notions which the learner will be able to handle. These refer to the concrete details of particular situations objects and actions. They are related to particular topics, and are indispensable for dealing with the 'here and now'.

7) the language forms which the learner will be able to use. These are the structures, words and phrases the learner will use in order to do all that has been specified. They are largely determined by considering language functions and notions separately and establishing the components which realise them in a particular language (the functional–notional approach). It is of course necessary to take into account the fact that a formal linguistic system has a coherent organisation and may involve obligatory grammatical categories which are not straightforwardly exponential (grammatical as opposed to natural gender, arbitrary declension and conjugation classes etc).

8) the degree of skill with which the learner will be able to perform. A learner who has acquired the resources set out above must still bring them into play in practical situations with sufficient fluency, appropriateness and accuracy for effective communication to take place. Whether a given level of performance is sufficient for effective communication depends very much on the interlocutor and the situation.

It was on the basis of this model that Dr J van Ek drew up the 'Threshold Level' specification which provided the first thorough-going, detailed, multi-dimensional specification of a communicative objective for a particular audience following the functional-notional approach embodied in the model. The T-level specification, which has been highly influential in subsequent syllabus design, attempts to formulate an explicit, worthwhile, realistic operational objective for learners who wish to be able to transact independently the business of everyday life in a foreign community and to build up basic human and social relationships with other speakers of the language in face-to-face communication. Following the publication of The threshold level in 1975, the same or similar learning objectives models for the specification of language were developed at other levels, for other audiences and other languages:

1) Waystage, by J van Ek and L G Alexander in association with M A Fitzpatrick for the Deutscher Volkshochschulverband (DVV) was published by the Council of Europe in 1977 and republished by Pergamon Press 1980. Waystage is a heavily pruned version of van Ek 1975, providing a sub-set of categories of high communicative priority with very simple exponents, suitable as an objective for a one-year

multi-media course. This specification provided the content syllabus for **Follow me**, the highly successful Anglo-German multi-media English course.

2) **Un niveau seuil**, by a team from the Centre de Recherche et Diffusion du Français (CREDIF) under the direction of D Coste (Council of Europe 1976) was largely based on The threshold level, but replaced language functions by a much more substantial categorisation of 'actes de parole', adding a semantics-based grammar following the principles of Guillaume and of Pottier. In addition, **Un niveau seuil** is not designed to serve the needs of one defined audience, but surveys the resources of French at a basic level, to be selected and applied to any one of a number of audiences according to the principles outlined in a special section and in an accompanying booklet by E Roulet: **Un niveau seuil, présentation et guide d'emploi**, Council of Europe 1977.

3) **A threshold level for modern language learning in schools**, by J van Ek, Longman 1976 is an adaptation of van Ek 1975 for use as an objective for secondary schools, mainly distinguished by differences in situations (roles, settings, topics) to take account of difference of age, the school environment and centres of interest, with all the differences in sub-categories and their exponents which result.

4) **Adaptation de 'Un niveau seuil' pour des contextes scolaires**, by a CREDIF team under the direction of L Porcher (Council of Europe, 1980) is an adaptation of Coste et al 1976 along similar lines.

5) **Un nivel umbral**, by P Slagter, Council of Europe, 1979 applies to Spanish the "classical" t-level model of van Ek 1975.

6) **Kontaktschwelle: Deutsch als Fremdsprache**, by a team from the Institut für deutsche Sprache, Universität Freiburg/Schweiz, under the direction of G Schneider (Council of Europe 1980 and republished by Langenscheidt 1982), integrates and develops the approaches of van Ek 1975 and Coste 1976. After a particularly clear theoretical discussion, Kontaktschwelle provides for German lists of Sprechakte, allgemeine Begriffe and spezifische Begriffe. A third part contains a classified and motivated inventory of grammatical and lexical structures.

7) **Livello soglia** by N Galli de'i Paratesi, Council of Europe, 1981, applies to Italian a model which draws elements from van Ek 1975, Coste 1976 and Schneider 1980.

8) **Tröskelnivå: Förslag till ninehåll och metod i den grundläggånde utbildninger i svenska fo vuxna invandrare**, by a team from Amu-center, Malmö under the direction of Bengt Sandström is a provisional document (1980) in which functional-notional principles are

used in the service of language for a particular audience (adult migrants). Contains a substantial introductory discussion of theoretical and methodological issues, followed by a full treatment of language functions and general notions, with an independent section on 'tröskelnivå för grammatik'.

9) A version for Danish, Et taerskelniveau for dansk (Jessen 1982), has been completed, building on proposals for Grundbaustein Dänisch of the Internationale Zertifikatskommission (IZK).

10) Un Nivell llindar, a T-level for Catalan, has been produced by a team in Barcelona, commissioned by the Generalitat de Catalunya.

11) A version for Dutch was requested by the Netherlands Government. A project steering committee was established under the chairmanship of Dr J van Ek. This version is now approaching draft stage.

12) The syllabuses for the Certificate and Grundbaustein examinations of the Internationale Zertifikatskommission in English, French, German, Spanish, Italian and Russian have been or are being drawn up or revised to form a harmonised system in accordance with the principles exemplified in the T-level documents.

13) Extensive use has been made of the functional-notional descriptive apparatus in many parts of the world, including in America, where it has been used to specify military tasks, Canada, for the activities of public service officials in a bilingual country and Australia, for immigrant 'on-arrival' programmes.

An attempt to produce a definitive model on this basis has been made by J Munby (1978). It differs from the van Ek model mainly in the addition of certain new dimensions, notably 'tone' to the descriptive framework. A more general account has been given by D Wilkins, whose paper 'The linguistic and situational content of the common core in a unit/credit system' in Trim et al 1980 was of seminal importance in the Council of Europe work, in his Notional syllabuses (1976).

The Threshold level and its successors were not conceived as syllabuses, in the sense of setting out a course of study and studying the content and sequence of lessons but rather as specifications of objectives, attempting to set out what a learning programme should lead to, rather than to set out the programme itself. The various syllabuses which have based themselves upon the T-level model may however be seen as 'output syllabuses'. They have proved useful in a number of ways. A highly explicit statement of a learning target provides teachers and students with something concrete and limited to aim at, the practical relevance of which can clearly be seen. Self-awareness and self-assessment are greatly facilitated, as is the growth of independence and increasing autonomy on the part of the students. A framework is provided within which teachers and students can negotiate their objectives, since functional-notional categories are meaningful to students from their previous linguistic experience. It is easier for students to discuss whether they should be able to offer and accept services, apologies, etc, or talk about things which might happen in the future, than to discuss whether the future conditional or the imperfect subjunctive should figure in the syllabus. The fact that methods and materials are left open allows for greater flexibility. The same specification can be used as an objective by students of different backgrounds and characteristics, who may come with different prior knowledge, have developed different study skills, have different preferred sense modalities or have different access to resources - including the services of teachers of varied professional backgrounds, skills and approaches.

In the eight years since the publication of The threshold level the model has been widely studied and used, and has received close critical attention. Early criticisms, from adherents of earlier structuralist and statistical specification models, fastened on details of vocabulary selection. Recent criticisms have been more fundamental and, though they have not diminished the usefulness of the components of the model, have shown it to require supplementation in certain respects. Brumfit (1980) and Widdowson (1978) have pointed out that as a characterisation of 'communicative competence' a listing of categories of utterances, however well organised, does not capture the strategies of interaction which enable speakers to co-operate towards a social goal, or to pursue competing interests. They should be supplemented by schemata of social action in which the particular speech acts find an appropriate place (Rehbein 1978). A very real problem remains how to characterise in any meaningful way the creativity and spontaneity of freely flowing conversation which is socially enjoyable and enriching without having any immediate practical goal. T-level provides an orderly classification of parts, but the whole dynamically evolving interaction, which is more than their sum, escapes our techniques, at least at present.

Many syllabuses, especially examination syllabuses, have attempted to specify global levels of communicative proficiency by incorporating the level decriptions devised by the Defense Language Institute or others derived from them. A number of such attempts are presented and evaluated in Trim (1980). These scales were originally intended as criteria for screening personnel and assessing their language proficiency. There are some dangers to be borne in mind when adapting them for the rather different task of specifying objectives. At lower levels, definitions are often in terms of incompetence. What the learner is not able to do characterises him rather than what he is able to do. Moreover, limited knowledge and operational range are equated with erratic and unskilful performance. Yet there is no reason why a beginner should start off with a heavy foreign accent carried over from the mother tongue, or fail to manipulate the language effectively within fairly narrow limits. It is hard to see how a foreign accent could be a learning objective! The assumption that the learner's pronunciation of the phonemes of the target language gradually approaches native values as he expands his knowledge of its grammar and vocabulary and his skill in conversation is psycholinguistically implausible. We are likely to find that the advanced learner has fixed his pronunciation habits and is impatiently resentful of continued correction at that level. A little practical phonetics while the language is still fresh enough to be interesting as sound, may be more acceptable and effective – provided that it does not become pedantic and gratuitously over-detailed. The scales are also usually based on the strict separation of the four so-called skills of reading, writing, listening and speaking. The four-skills analysis not only tends to encourage a deceptive parallelism in their decription, but also gives no scope for showing the almost necessarily unequal development of sub-skills (e.g in speech: word-finding, sentence formulation, sound production, fluent catenation of strings of sounds and control of stress and intonation).

(Note that each successive level *subsumes* those prior to it.
Note also that it is not *necessary* to approach "Waystage" via "survival")

"ambilingual"	7.	Acts linguistically in a way operationally indistinguishable from native speakers with corresponding personal and social characteristics.
"comprehensive mastery"	6.	Is unhampered by linguistic deficiencies in conducting a normal social and personal life. Has productive and receptive control over all exponents needed to express functional and notional complexity of transactions and interactions likely to be encountered, as well as politeness conventions and full range of styles.
"effective proficiency"	5.	Is able to use language flexibly and effectively in normal situations, including emotional, allusive and joking usage. Controls formal and colloquial styles as well as degrees of politeness. Can follow complex discourse and conversations between native speakers in familiar style (not special slangs).
"adequate response normally encountered"	4.	Is able to find some adequate response to the great majority of social situations normally encountered including those not specifically foreseen. Can produce and understand straightforward narrative and descriptive discourse and chain of reasoned argument, and adjust to the changes of direction, style and emphasis normally found in conversation.
"threshold"	3.	Is able to participate simply but effectively in the range of social situations necessary to the normal everyday transactional and interactional needs of temporary visitors by producing and recognizing simple exponents of the functional and notional categories concerned under normal conversational conditions involving a foreign learner.
"waystage"	2.	Is able to deal with a limited range of very common social situations, transactional and interactional, e.g. by producing and recognizing the simplest exponents of the notional and functional categories concerned in the required combinations appropriately and intelligibly, given goodwill and favourable conditions.
"survival"	1.	Is able to secure satisfaction of limited needs in highly predictable and easily recognizable transactional situations, e.g. by producing and recognizing a set of words and short phrases learnt by heart, and by making a limited number of lexical substitutions in fixed sentence frames.

Figure 1

For these reasons (leaving aside the impressionistic and evaluative nature of the terms used), proficiency scales are to be accorded only a limited place in syllabus construction. They do, however, play a useful role in providing statements intelligible to learners, employers, administrators and the general public. As an example, Figure 1 reproduces the scale suggested for 'social skills' in Trim (1980) p 35.

The development of the learner as a communicator is also not the only responsibility of adult education, any more than of the child at school. We have already mentioned the development of the learner as a learner in referring to the development of self-awareness, self-reliance and study skills. Participation in an organised taught course is (or should be) one episode in a long-term learning process. The success of the learning programme is to be judged not only on the basis of the learner's increased communicative competence and proficiency, but also on the extent that he has progressed towards autonomy – the ability and willingness to take charge of his own further learning. If the student remains teacher-dependent, then the end of the course signifies the end of learning and the slower or faster loss of the skills and knowledge acquired (Lambert and Freed 1982). Furthermore, a language course, no less than any other part of adult education, has among its aims the general development and enrichment of the student's individual personality, cultural development and social education as an effective member of a cooperating social group. Autonomy is <u>not</u> solipsism!

In fact a syllabus has to be informed by broad educational aims rooted in a coherent educational philosophy. It is of course possible to include these in a statement of terminal objectives, but it is no longer possible to remain open on methodology, to maintain a separation of ends and means. It is a question of promoting and facilitating the development of the learner from moment to moment during class meetings, and from one such meeting to the next, whether as communicator, as learner, as social being or as an individual personality.

We have already considered communicative objectives at some length in relation to T-level as a terminal objective. What of the process whereby this objective is to be reached? Here we have first to consider the relation of knowledge and skills to communication. Communication may take place directly, in face-to-face (or 'ear-to-ear', e.g. telephonic) interaction, or indirectly through communication media (newspapers, books, films, recordings, radio, TV, public announcements etc). In either case a message is formulated, encoded and produced by a sender, transmitted by means of some physical medium, and perceived, identified, understood and interpreted by a receiver. For communication to be effective, both parties draw on their understanding of the language concerned as a symbolic system linguistic competence) and the conventions governing its use (communicative competence) as well as their understanding of the extra-linguistic parameters of the situation in which the message is embedded, including background knowledge, together with the general principles of social behaviour (social competence).

In addition to these different 'competencies' or aspects of know-ledge, the language user must have developed the mental and physical skills necessary to act as sender and/or receiver. In indirect com-munication an individual is called upon to act only as one or other at any one time. In direct communication, the rapid switching (and to some extent overlapping) of roles makes further demands. We have to plan our response whilst still listening to our partner. In general, productive skills involving stimulus-free recall are more demanding than receptive recognition skills. The processing of speech as it comes to the ear is more demanding than the production or perception of a written text, which can be scanned or edited at comparative leisure. (This principle is qualified by the fact that reading and writing come later than speech in the development of the individual and in the history of society. To that extent they are ways of representing speech, secondary activities rather than a primary mode of communication.)

Neither knowledge nor skills are ends in themselves, but prerequis-ites for effective communicative action in pursuit of social goals in given situations. However, the order of presupposition raises a number of questions of teaching and learning method as well as for testing. Traditionally, knowledge of the linguistic system is presented to the learner piecemeal, in the putative 'logico-develop-mental' sequence mentioned above. Tests are administered ('discrete-point testing') to ensure that the teaching point has been 'learnt'. This may take the form of classroom question-and-answer tests, or pencil-and-paper tests involving multiple-choice questions, gap-filling exercises or sentence translation. The aim is to confirm the acquisition of knowledge. Though this can only be done by eliciting a response which must take the form of some activity, the activity is of no consequence except as evidence of knowledge. Success lies in the avoidance of error. Research into classroom teaching (Lunt and Trim 1982) shows that pupil activity in schools is almost exclusively of this kind. Language learning becomes almost entirely a matter of pressing on from one teaching point to the next along the prescribed path - what I have elsewhere (Trim 1980 p 3) termed the Euclidean or gradus ad Parnassum approach, pointing out that the path is littered with corpses and the summit scaled by very few.

Too little time is generally devoted to the progressive development of skills and their application to the solution of communication problems. There are many reasons for the neglect of that process. For one thing it demands a good deal of time, to be spent in active participation by students in a way which is incompatible with the traditional teacher-centred classroom. Students are simultaneously active in a way the teacher cannot control or monitor. The resultant gain in communicative proficiency is difficult to evaluate - and not at all by the cheap if not cheerful error-counting methods listed above. Furthermore, as was pointed out earlier the de facto syllabus underlying the work of the class is likely to be a textbook, containing concocted texts/dialogues with teaching points seeded through them, followed by drill exercises to consolidate the learning of these points, to be worked through in time for students to sit for an examination which in turn resembles an obstacle course with points deducted for each stumble. The reasons why this system is still so widely followed are readily understandable, being ultimately financial. To break out of the system despite these constraints is difficult for an individual teacher. From an under-resourced, underpaid, statusless, part-time teacher in adult education with no professional training the necessary awareness and determination are hardly to be expected. To produce a teaching force able to meet the responsibilities outlined above, the professional training and status of teachers in adult education must be raised to equal that of teachers in schools. Strong and sustained pressure will be necessary to overcome the political and financial obstacles, Meanwhile the explicit process syllabus allied to multi-media course organisation and in-service teacher training affords the possibility of a decisive move forward, especially if appropriate forms of testing, evaluation and recognised examination qualification are made available to both students and teachers.

As opposed to the output syllabus, the process syllabus quantifies the learning process, guides the learner's progress in terms of competencies, skills and communication activities, continuously gearing ends to means. How far can process specification be taken? It would seem at present somewhat premature to establish a methodological orthodoxy and to close down options. A number of proposed methods coexist, vigorously supported by their proponents and adherents. For instance, one strong current of opinion (Krashen, Lyatowsky) favours a period of exposure to language in a relaxed atmosphere before any productive demands are placed upon the learner. Dodson proposes a regular alternation of 'medium-oriented' and 'message-oriented' activities (e.g. that whenever a piece of language is learnt it should be put to a genuine communicative use without delay). Some propose a treatment for receptive activities, using problem-solving techniques on authentic material (i.e. not specially composed or edited), radically different from the use of limited controlled productive activities in conversation. Some still favour a teacher-dominated rapid-fire whole class stimulus-response method, others much more varied individual pair and group work. Many keep to the orthodoxy of presentation, practice, exploitation and recapitulation. Much appears still to depend upon personal qualities of teachers: patience, warmth, commitment, empathy, clarity of exposition and explanation, pitching demands on students at a high, but attainable level, encouraging, recognising and rewarding effort, etc (York University 1982). Enthusiasm and the 'Hawthorne effect' will themselves go a long way to ensuring success. Careful experimentation with a proper control on variables is extremely difficult, so that at present it may be best to monitor the results of taking up various options and not rush to judgement. This is not to advocate a flaccid relativism. Some practices are pernicious and, where that is established, the fact should be stated loudly and clearly. Otherwise we should keep an open mind and avoid dogmatism.

A distinction must of course be made between a course syllabus and a guideline syllabus. The course syllabus is established for a particular programme with a particular group of learners. It may be set up by a course designer, or negotiated between teachers and learners. In either case it necessarily involves fairly detailed planning and incorporates a series of decisions which inevitably close down options. A guideline syllabus prescribes (whether in a mandatory or advisory way) aims, objectives and methods for the many different teaching/ learning situations it attempts to coordinate. It treads delicately between support and coercion. In the approach to adult education assumed here, its role is best seen as articulation of choice rather than imposition of authority. Options should be closed on other people's behalf only if one is very sure of one's ground! In practice, the issue is far from clear-cut, but some situations dictate the approaches to be used. Whereas a self-intructional programme has to be highly explicit in its instructions to the learner, class-teacher-based systems do well to leave scope for a more flexible interaction between students and teachers. A multi-media system, which attempts to use all available resources in an appropriate way, will find room for both approaches.

In a trivial sense, virtually all teaching/learning systems are multi-media, with the possible exception of an unfortunate learner trying to work alone with a textbook (even here dedication and intelligence can achieve surprising results). 'Chalk and talk' defines two separate channels of communication, visual and auditory. However, the term is more commonly used for more complex systems using a wide range of channels usually, but not necessarily, led by public broadcasting media. Figure 2 on page 49 shows the various resources which may be available to a learner in a multi-media system. It is doubtful whether any teaching system will employ all the resources shown. Which are used will depend on their availability and the nature of the learning situation in relation to the characteristics of the media.

Let us first consider the public broadcasting media, TV and radio. Television programmes are inherently expensive. There are few channels, with intense competition for audiences. Programme controllers must look to maximise the audience, aiming to capture the interest of the general public rather than satisfy specialist needs. Since

INTERACTION BETWEEN LEARNER AND LEARNING ENVIRONMENT

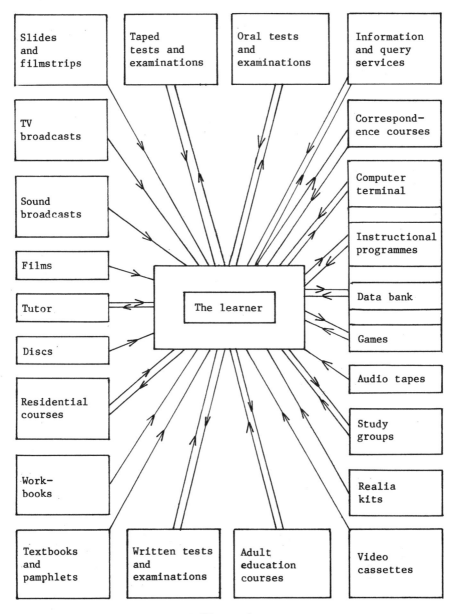

Figure 2

the target audiences are much larger than the numbers which do (or
perhaps can) participate in LEA classes, it is to the home viewer
rather than the institutionalised student the TV programmes are
normally directed. Of course, some relatively small audiences, such
as the handicapped and their relatives, may be given priority for
social reasons at off-peak periods. Nevertheless, the decision to
seek a mass audience of home listeners can be justified
independently of the financial constraint. Most young adults have
now had some exposure to language learning. In many cases they have
given up at about 14 with little sense of achievement and often an
acute sense of inferiority and communicative incompetence. They are
unlikely to return to institutional adult education unless their
motivation is rekindled. TV is the only medium through which they
are likely to be accessible.

To capture its audience it is, however, necessary to satisfy expectations either through entertainment value, or through the current
affairs or 'world about us' connection. In either case a comparably
high standard of production and presentation is imperative, and if
the programmes can bring wider sections of the public to enlarge
their international awareness, to accept the reality and value of
other cultures, to accept other languages as valid ways of encoding
experience and conducting daily life, they will already have made a
valuable contribution to the modernisation of British society. But,
of course, it is one thing to be sensitised to a language in use and
to be motivated to learn, but actually to learn a language is a
rather different matter. At an earlier stage, when the various media
operated in isolation, radio and TV producers and authors attempted
to incorporate all aspects of teaching into their programmes, which
were seen as miniature lessons. Books and recordings were issued and
some care was taken to make it possible for students to work
systematically combining broadcast materials with support materials.
Nevertheless, the contribution which different media could make was
not so carefully explored in Britain as it was, say, in Finland,
where, for obvious reasons, they did not attempt to make independent
programmes but devoted its limited resources to embedding programmes
bought from abroad in a less expensive multi-media framework and
strengthening the organisation at the receivers' end.

The decision by the BBC in 1973 to integrate radio and TV components
in its forthcoming 'Kontakte' series has led over the last decade to
an increasingly purposive assessment of respective functions. TV has
made more and more use of structured and controlled naturalism,
filming on location ordinary native speakers in unscripted but
rehearsed and skilfully edited interviews, in carefully selected
situations representative on the one hand of the culture concerned
and its human impact upon its members and on the other of the human,
social and business contacts in which foreigners are characteristi-
cally involved. The visual element has been fully exploited to
convey such non-verbal aspects of culture as setting, gesture and

facial expression, and to introduce the increased redundancy that can enable meaning to be grasped without sacrificing authenticity of speech. This direction of policy has proved remarkably successful. The viewing figures for Buongiorno Italia, which contains no English and no discursive teaching, have reached the highest level yet achieved for language broadcasting in this country. The figure of 1.8 million viewers, for programme 11, the first programme of the second term, was reported in January 1983.

Meanwhile, the radio component has overcome the stilted language and funereal routines of the fifties and sixties and has learnt to exploit its intimacy and immediacy, its ability to claim close concentration upon auditory sensation free from visual distraction, its liberation of the visual imagination.

Books and recordings were introduced primarily as a means of providing the texts, written and spoken respectively, of the broadcasts. It is now being realised that, though the booklets now stand high in the paperback charts and the cassettes achieve volume sales, the purchasers constitute a special sub-audience, with greater independence, drive and motivation for language learning than the purely viewing or listening audience. Consequently it is possible to transfer the burden of systematic, progressive language learning to the individualised media, where the student has control over the mode of use. A book can be skipped through or intensively studied by turns, reading can be repeated ad lib. Cassettes - though not to the same extent discs - can equally be replayed in different modes.

Filmstrips have long been available as a visual presentation device by the 'structuro-global audio-visual method' of Guberina and Rivenc. c. They can easily be produced as a spin-off from TV programmes. They can jog the memory, but lack the dynamism of TV (or film) and are much more restricted in their role, being more akin to book illustrations (into which they have in fact been frequently converted).

Recently, greater emphasis has been laid on exposing and accustoming learners to the authentic use of language as opposed to the use of specially constructed textual material. Newspapers, magazines, advertising and publicity materials of all kinds are often produced by highly skilled communication technicians who manipulate the language in order to achieve a range of rhetorical effects (bold simplicity, stark antitheses, repetitive structures etc) which lend themselves to ready use for language learning purposes. Partly for reasons of copyright, partly because ephemeral topicality and fresh spontaneity are part of the attraction of such materials, they are likely to be provided from time to time by particular teachers and classes rather than forming part of a centrally provided kit. The British Council film Using magazine pictures gives a detailed account of one way to exploit this resource.

51

Recent technical developments have produced devices which, as they become more widely available, are likely greatly to extend the potential of multi-media learning systems. Videotape machines are now widely installed in adult education centres and are penetrating the home market in considerable numbers. Recording off-air is permitted to educational institutions under certain published conditions. The Anglo-German multi-media English course Follow me was recently made the occasion for equipping all German Volkshochschulen with VTRs and establishing their right to copy off-air. The value of the VTR is very plain. Once recorded, a TV programme is not a linear nonce event, but an audio-visual text which can be replayed an indefinite number of times, segmented, studied intensively and otherwise manipulated under the flexible control of teacher or student. Programmes designed with this use in view can be denser and less repetitious. The extent to which this trend can be followed will, however, depend a good deal on the producers' skill in producing programmes which will both appeal to the semi-casual home listener and stand up to intensive use and re-use.

The future of the much-heralded video disc is still far from clear. In principle, its huge channel capacity would make it possible for very large numbers of still frames to replace a short moving film sequence. These frames can contain extensive reference materials such as a grammar and a dictionary, exercise materials banks organised into branching programmes and programmes to be fed into microcomputers. Particular frames can be much more rapidly located in the two dimensions of the disc than the one of the tape. Clearly, the videodisc is an extremely powerful information source. An equally high level of initial investment is needed to get the system off the ground and the commercial issues which will determine whether the videodisc as a purely reproduction device will establish itself in the face of the record-and-replay VTR present an unresolved issue.

Small personal computers are already here to stay. It is likely that BBC will in the not too distant future broadcast programmes recordable off-air for use on its own micro-computer. These may well include programmes issued in connection with future BBC multi-media language teaching series. What will such programmes have to offer? In the first instance, it seems likely that most traditional kinds of exercise can be converted into computer form. The gain will be in the machine's immediate response and the possibility of giving exercises a more imaginitive, game-like character. The principal drawback at the present time is the inability of computers to respond to a speech input. Several speech synthesis programmes are now available, so that a micro-computer can already be programmed to speak to the learner. It is a matter of dispute whether the quality of speech is acceptable for language learning purposes. Speech recognition is however still out of reach — perhaps the most important and intractable problem in articificial intelligence research at the present time. Until it is solved the learner cannot speak to the machine.

Interaction is greatly slowed down by the need to type in responses and in any case many may feel that methodologically we have moved one step forward and two steps back from the language laboratory! It is perhaps better to concentrate on the virtues of the micro-computer, such as its flexibility and its ability to involve an otherwise isolated learner in an interactive situation. We have then to encourage the application of good programming minds to optimising the exploitation of strengths and minimising limitations. A regular newsletter 'Callboard' is now available giving news of developments in computer-assisted language learning (CALL) and the present state of the art is surveyed by Davies and Higgins in CILT Information Guide 22: <u>Computers, language, and language learning</u>.

As figure 2 shows, the above discussion does not exhaust the potentialities of multi-media language learning systems. Among other devices that can be mentioned is the telephone. Pre-recorded messages can range from news bulletins, songs and stories to 'exercises for the day'. 'Phone friends' could perhaps be organised as an alternative to pen friends. A number of phone-in tutorial query services have already been organised in connection with broadcast programmes. Local radio has used the phone-in programme as a way of making answers to queries more generally useful - most people have similar problems.

It remains to consider the teacher and the classroom as elements in a multi-media system. Communication is a social skill. Some of its prerequisites can be learnt by studying alone, but the skilled activity of social cooperation through speech can only develop in company, in the give-and-take of personal interaction. That is the essential role of class-work in a multi-media system. It has frequently been pointed out that the main effect of multi-media operation on teachers is to change their role from that of presenter and monitor to that of manager and therapist. In adult education it may generally be assumed (with certain reservations) that students will wish to act as mature and independent persons. The teacher may then ecape from always having to present the language itself in immaculate form and personally checking every productive language act by every student. Instead, he or she can organise the students' access to different kinds of material appropriate to different stages and levels leaving the presentation to the different vehicles devised for that purpose. The teacher is also left freer to oversee the progress of students. Some of them will present relatively few problems. Others may have blocks and require closer individual attention before these blocks can be cleared. The teacher has also an enhanced role as animator, orchestrating the varied activities, engaging individuals, pairs and groups and the whole class by turns as modern communicative methods require. As has been pointed out earlier, not all the activities can be watched over; too many are taking place simultaneously. That does not mean that the teacher has no control over what is happening, or is an impotent bystander. New methods of control are made possible by closer task specification and self-assessment or mutual assessment by the learners whether or not the task has been accomplished, together with a reporting-back procedure.

In brief, a multi-media learning system offers the learner access to a range of learning situations, in which he can develop an increasing independence of action as communicator, as learner, as member of a social group and as an individual personality. Syllabus development is an aid to learners in structuring their efforts to that end, and to teachers in helping them to do so.

REFERENCES

AUSTIN, J C: How to do things with words. 2nd edn. ed. by J O Urmson and Marina Sbisà. Oxford: 1975.

BALDEGGER, M, M MULLER, G SCHNEIDER and A NÄF: Kontaktschwelle: Deutsch als Fremdsprache. Strasbourg: Council of Europe, 1980; Munich: Langenscheidt, 1982.

BRUMFIT, C J: Problems and principles in English teaching. Oxford: Pergamon Press, 1980.

CARTIER, Francis A and others: Method for determining language objectives and criteria: final report of recommendations; a study ... for the Defense Language Institute Foreign Language Center. New York: Development & Evaluation Associates Inc, 1979.

CENTRE DE RECHERCHE ET D'ETUDE POUR LA DIFFUSION DU FRANÇAIS (CREDIF): Le français fondamental: éléments de bibliographie analytique. Saint-Cloud: CREDIF, 1970.

COSTE, D, J COURTILLON, V FERENCZI, M MARTINS-BALTAR, E PAPO and E ROULET: Un niveau seuil. Strasbourg: Council of Europe, 1976; Paris?: Hatier, 1976.

DAVIES, G and J J HIGGINS: Computers, language and language learning. London: Centre for Information on Language Teaching and Research, 1983. (Information Guide 22.)

DEUTSCHER VOLKSHOCHSCHUL-VERBAND and GOETHE-INSTITUT: Das Zertifikat Deutsch als Fremdsprache. Bonn-Bad Godesberg, Munich: Deutscher Volkshochschul-Verban e.V. and Goethe-Institut zur Pflege der deutschen Sprache im Ausland und zur Förderung der internationalen kulturellen Zusammenarbeit e.V., 1972.

van EK, J A: The threshold level of modern language learning in schools. Harlow: Longman, 1977.

van EK, J A: Waystage English (grammatical inventory by L G Alexander in association with M A Fitzpatrick). Strasbourg: Council of Europe, 1977; Oxford, New York etc: Pergamon Press, 1980.

van EK, J A and L G ALEXANDER: Threshold Level English. Oxford: Pergamon Press, 1980.

FRANCE, MINISTERE DE L'EDUCATION NATIONALE: Le français fondamental. Paris: 1959.

GALLI de' PARATESI, N: Livello soglia. Strasbourg: Council of Europe, 1981.

JESSEN, J: Et taerskelniveau for dansk. Strasbourg: Council of Europe, 1982.

LAMBERT, Richard D and Barbara F FREED (eds): The loss of language skills. Rowley, Mass: Newbury House, 1982.

MUNBY, John L: Communicative syllabus design: a socio-linguistic model for defining the content of purpose-specific language programmes. Cambridge: Cambridge University Press, 1978.

PORCHER, L, M HUART and F MARIET: Adaptation de 'Un niveau seuil' pour des contextes scolaires. Strasbourg: Council of Europe, 1980; Paris : Hatier, 1982.

SANDSTRÖM, Bengt and others: Tröskelnivå: Förslag till innehåll och metod i den grundläggande utbildningen i svenska för vuxna invandrare. Malmö: Amu-center, nd.

SEARLE, John R
Speech acts: an essay in the philosophy of language. Cambridge: Cambridge University Press, 1969.

SHANNON, Clark E and Warren WEAVER: The mathematical theory of communication. Urbana: University of Illinois Press, 1959.

SLAGTER, P J: Un nivel umbral. Strasbourg: Council of Europe, 1979.

THORNDIKE, Edward L and Irving LORGE: The teacher's word book of 30,000 words. New York: Columbia University, 1952.

TRIM, J L M: Developing a unit/credit scheme of adult language learning. Strasbourg: Council of Europe, 1978; Oxford, New York etc: Pergamon Press, 1980.

TRIM, J L M, R RICHTERICH, J van EK and D WILKINS: Systems development in adult language learning. Strasbourg: Council of Europe, 1973; Oxford, New York etc: Pergamon Press, 1980.

55

WIDDOWSON, H G: Teaching languages as communication. Oxford: Oxford Univeristy Press, 1978.

WILKINS, David A: Notional syllabuses: a taxonomy and its reference to foreign language curriculum development. Oxford: Oxford University Press, 1976.

YORK UNIVERSITY LANGUAGE TEACHING CENTRE: Modern language teachers in action. York: 1982.

ZIPF, George Kingsley: The psycho-biology of language: an introduction to dynamic philology. Cambridge, Mass.: M.I.T. Press, 1965.

IN THE CLASSROOM

John Langran

'Bonjour mesdames, bonjour mesdemoiselles, bonjour messieurs!' So now you have a group of people meeting you once a week, giving up what is for many of them valuable time, and paying a fee to have you try to help them learn a language. They are probably quite a mixed group, coming to the class for different reasons and possibly in a not-too-well-graded group. Some may be tired after work, others nervous at returning to 'school'. Some may want to dominate and others seem to want to hide. Some may be really good at learning languages, while others may have had little success in the past.

Whether you are an experienced teacher of adults, of school children or an inexperienced teacher who has landed this job by virtue of being a native speaker, each new group of adult students will pose a new challenge.

What are you actually going to do? Let us start by looking at extracts from interviews with a number of adults who attended day or evening classes with a fair amount of success.

-    'There were three reasons why I came - firstly, coming to a new city I wanted an opportunity to meet people; secondly, I have

57

always been interested in foreign countries and a good way to learn more about them is through the languages, and thirdly, I have a good deal of spare time and so it helps fill my evenings usefully.'

- 'It's been businesslike and professional, but in a friendly way; I mean you can come and enjoy yourself, you can have a good evening, as well as learning something. There hasn't been anything 'intensive' about it, but we've still got quite a lot done.'

- 'I've enjoyed the company, and I've also improved my French no end. The atmosphere in the classroom has made all the difference in the world. I'm so much older than the other students, but I've been accepted as a contemporary which has made a big difference. I just couldn't come if I was regarded as a fuddy-duddy. I can't speak too highly of the tutors either. They have been sociable and kind but at the same time they have got on with the work.'

- 'I think it's the atmosphere of the centre, because they are all so very friendly right from the moment you come in to register, right from the very start. You're welcomed in, and everybody smiles, you're on Christian name terms before you know where you are...'

- 'I wanted a current, colloquial French, so that I could talk to French people in an everyday situation. I go to France two or three times a year, it's my hobby in retirement. A more academic approach wouldn't have helped, I've finished with that...'

- 'I think it's more important for me to be able to understand French people speaking than anything else.'

- 'In the classroom, although she is very nice about it, she really makes us work quite hard, but it's not boring work, we have to actually do things ourself in the language most of the time.'

It is not difficult to summarise what contributed to the success of the classes these people attended:

(1) The atmosphere in the classroom dependent on the room itself, the personality and approach of the teacher, and relationships with other people in the group and the centre as a whole.

(2) The perceived practical relevance of the teaching programme and the methods used. The sense of achievement and purposefulness, and the emphasis on communication and activity in class.

In this chapter I shall attempt to give an analysis of successful practice in Adult Education classes based on these principles, and showing what practical steps teachers can take to achieve these ends.

ATMOSPHERE

It is important for you to encourage a friendly welcoming atmosphere in a classroom that also evokes the country whose language is being studied. Your group is likely to have varying memories of school-days, and a return to the classroom will not be easy for all of them.

The importance of a good classroom organisation has been mentioned earlier in this volume. A circular or semi-circular seating arrangement will give you two major advantages: the room will at once look less like a schoolroom and the people will all be able to see each other properly. From time to time it is likely that you will find other seating arrangements useful, (e.g. for group work), but a flexible arrangement based on a circle or horse-shoe is generally most popular.

The friendliness of the atmosphere will depend on everyone present, but most importantly on the teacher who will probably set the tone. It is useful for you to know everyone by name, and you will probably start to use first names for most students fairly soon in the course. It is important to greet people at the beginning of the lesson as much as you can. It is also vital to give people the chance to get to know each other early in the course. If it is possible to help the group establish a friendly atmosphere of mutual help and concern this can only be to the long-term good of the group:

- People may give each other lifts in bad weather;
- They may loan each other cassettes or video recordings of useful material;
- They may form a social group that meets perhaps after the class around the theme of learning the language, and organises visits to restaurants etc. You may find there is a willing social secretary in the group, and that once the initial suggestions have been made by you the group takes over;
- They may even visit absent friends at home or in hospital and keep them abreast of what is going on in the class;
- Perhaps most important, given a friendly atmosphere, they are more likely to discuss their learning and their needs with each other and with you, and give you more useful feedback on the work you are doing.

It is difficult to prescribe a way of generating such an atmosphere in classes, as so much depends on the personalities of the people concerned. Not everyone, of course, will want to do anything more than come to a class. You may, however, be able to lay the foundations for such an atmosphere in your classes by certain fairly simple devices:

- Make sure that names are used in class;
- Make sure that the group is able to sit together at coffee break;
- Do not dominate all the time. Let members of the group take the initiative from time to time;
- Keep people abreast of what is going on. For example, when you have an apology for absence, pass it on;
- Possibly suggest that people share cassette recordings for use at home;
- You may perhaps instigate informal discussion of how people are getting on and to what extent they are benefitting from the course.

One possible danger in the generating of a good social atmosphere is that your group might give the appearance of being a clique and newcomers might be put off. If this looks likely, perhaps have a quiet word with a group member who is able to look after the newcomer for a while. Another danger is that any extra-curricular activities may be an embarrassment to people who are unable to or do not want to participate. If an excursion to a restaurant is being planned, for example at the end of a term, bear in mind that there may be people in the group who cannot afford it. Try to avoid the situation where people are seen to be 'left out'.

The second important point about the creation of atmosphere is the need to create in your classroom a feeling for the language that is being learnt. If this is French, you might:

- Play a cassette of café music as students arrive and at breaks;
- Put up a few simple notices, e.g. 'Défense de fumer', 'Priorité aux handicappés de guerre' etc;
- Perhaps bring a bottle of wine with a French flag to go on the table at the front of your room;
- Bring a map of France for the wall;
- Put up some posters or postcards, if the regular room user does not mind, and encourage students to contribute if they can.

These ideas are intended for teachers working once or twice a week in a room that is not their own. If you have a regular room for teaching the same language there should be no problem about creating this atmosphere, but make sure that displays are changed regularly to keep the atmosphere fresh and exciting.

Linked with the creation of atmosphere is, of course, the question of the extent to which English can be used in the classroom. The most common agreement is that it is helpful to use English where you can save a lot of time – explaining the rules of a particular game, explaining a trick of pronunciation, or a peculiarity of grammar or vocabulary, as well as explaining and discussing aims. At other times the teacher should be able to conduct the proceedings entirely in the language being learnt. Certainly all greetings, pleasantries, often-used instructions, etc can be used right from the start and can begin to give the student an acquired vocabulary which in due course can become quite substantial.

To summarise this section, the atmosphere which developes in groups will depend to an extent on the personalities of the people involved. The teacher can, however, use several tactics and devices to enable the development of a caring, purposeful atmosphere that evokes the language being taught and can greatly enhance the quality of work in the class.

LINGUISTIC AIMS

I remember conducting an amateurish survey of students enrolling for languages classes at an adult evening class centre. In reply to the question, 'Why are you joining the class?', every member of a particular German group said, 'To learn German'. When questioned a little more deeply on the subject most adults will tell you their primary aim is to learn to speak. The age of the study purely from books is passing. We now use radio, tape, video, computer-aided learning and so on. People are more likely to be mobile and are learning languages for travel, whether for work, holiday or family reasons. Reasons for choosing language courses are well documented in Teaching languages (1), and general reasons have been discussed earlier in this volume. On the whole the idea in people's minds is to learn to speak the language.

If we analyse this more closely, we see that what people need is to be able to survive and make a contribution in an environment where the language is being spoken. To do this at all levels you need to be able to understand more than you can say. For example, if you are in a town in Spain wanting to find the post office, and ask in perfect Spanish, 'Por favor,   hay correos por aqui?', this is of absolutely no use to you unless you are going to be able to understand the reply. Here the difficulties start because there are a number of possible replies ranging from the anticipated, 'Siga todo recto, a unos 400 metros a mano izquierda hay correos a la derecha' to the reply from the person you asked who happened to be deaf, 'Lo siento soy un puco sordo en e oido izquierdo. Por favor repitalo'.

The practical point is that if in your learning of Spanish you have concentrated your time and energy on cultivating a near-perfect pronunciation and intonation you will have spent less time on practising coping with possible replies.

For practical purposes then, when we talk about learning to speak a language, we need to put great emphasis on being able to understand replies, which means learning to recognise a larger number of words and structures than we are able to speak, and this must be borne in mind when courses and lessons are being planned.

The second important point in a discussion of aims is that we are dealing with groups of adults of varying ages whose individual and collective experience of the world is likely to be quite considerable and in many spheres is obviously likely to exceed that of the teacher. You will not be teaching in a day school where by definition you are of a higher 'status' than your students. By the time people reach a certain maturity it is quite clear that they know how they are able to do things. They develop specific strategies for learning and are able to discard more easily items which are not useful to them. The patronising teacher might say that they become 'set in their ways', but the vital key to smooth management of adult groups is not to patronise. The skilful teacher is able to harness the students' awareness of the learning processes that are going on as a means of increasing progress and individual and group motivation:

- In general discussion of how they are getting on, students can give each other useful tips on how they learn and can seek guidance from the teacher.

- If there is discussion of aims and methods the student who 'wants grammar' may well see that he is on his own in this respect and renew his efforts to cope with an unfamiliar way of learning. I remember clearly a discussion in a second-year French group in which a student in his 20's was insisting that he really wanted to learn to write French. When quizzed on this by other students in a challenging manner, which I as a teacher would never have dared to use, he admitted that this was, in fact, to be able to send letters to his girl-friend in the suburbs of Paris. 'Why don't you write in English and let her write in French?' suggested a middle-aged businessman, veteran of several international conferences. 'Why not send each other cassette recordings?' said a wry gentleman at the end of the coffee table, and pulled out his pocket dictaphone, then a novelty, to demonstrate. A few weeks later my French class had started a regular exchange of tapes and letters with an English class in the north of France, an exchange which has since led to several visits and friendships, all due to a student who nearly left the group because he thought he needed to learn to write the language.

- If there is ongoing discussion of the learning process, this can enable you as a teacher to explain your reasons for doing things in class in a particular way. You may perhaps use my earlier

Spanish example as an argument against spending too much time on pronunciation. You may be able to explain your reasons for choosing a particular game or activity in preference to the drilled exercises in the course book, or your reasons for not letting people look at the text when you play the tape recording. You may be able to demonstrate the value of reading at home or listening to French radio while doing the ironing. My favourite example of this is the learning of poetry. It is easy to demonstrate how much more easily you can remember a short poem or song than ordinary sentences. By spending a few minutes on a new short poem, song or catchy proverb each week, a group can soon notice the unexpected bonus of an increased vocabulary, interest and 'feel' for the language.

The danger of open discussion of aims and methods in an adult group is that the members will disagree with each other and you and form loyalties for and against particular ways of doing things. And once opinions have been stated people may find it difficult to 'back-down'. The most insistent and persistent contributors to such discussion are also likely to be people who prefer more formal methods and are resisting new trends. For these reasons, I am not in favour of introducing too much discussion about teaching methods before the group has established itself and a certain sympathetic unity has formed; and after a few weeks, of course, it is likely that your group will already be feeling the benefits of the methods you are using, which is likely to preempt the discussion. Of course it can be most useful for you, for example, to attend the enrolment session in order to be able to assess the needs of the majority of the group. It is also extremely useful for you to have as much say as you possibly can in the advertising and description of your course in the prospectus. (See Chapter 5.) The danger to beware of is in asking a new group what kind of language course they want to follow. If you are lucky and they all want roughly the same thing then you are likely to gain a certain increase in motivation which can only help. But if the group divides into factions who appear to want totally different things, possibly bringing to the argument sad experiences from previous classes where they have failed, then attitudes may harden and the majority of the group may only become frustrated at spending too much time talking about it and not enough time getting on with the course.

To summarise this section, many people tend to have quite strong opinions as to the 'right' and 'wrong' way to learn a language. Adult groups with a large age-range, varying previous experiences and differing motivations, are likely to need careful management in order to come to a compromise about learning methods.

This being said, the majority of adults coming to our courses will have a prime need to be able to speak and understand the spoken language in practical situations, and as the group develops it is

normally possible to establish a consensus of opinion around these
aims, with the additional motivation of a group of mature people
keen to discuss their needs.

THE COURSE

The choice of course material for a particular group is either made
by the responsible person in a centre in consultation with tutors,
or the choice is left to the teacher. The teacher can decide to
leave the decision to the group when it has formed, or it may even
be the policy of the centre that this should be done. The advantages
and disadvantages of discussing the course with the group in the
early stages have been considered in the previous section. Several.
practical points can be added here:

- If a teacher likes a particular book he or she usually works
  better with it;
- If a particular course has been chosen in advance this does help
  enormously with enrolment and pre-course advertising;
- If there is a problem over availability of course books, this
  can be minimised by ordering in advance, and if students can buy
  their book at the enrolment session they are able to feel that
  they are getting off to a good start and have something to get
  their teeth into.

On the other hand:

- Beware of choosing a course book that your students may consider
  too expensive;
- Beware of choosing a book inappropriate to the needs of the
  learner;
- Beware of choosing something the students may have used before,
  as can easily happen in classes with non-beginners or faux-débutants.

With these practical considerations in mind we can look at the basic
question of what type of course to choose. From the previous section
it is clear that speaking and understanding the spoken language are
the main concerns of adult learners, and for this reason the recent
output of the BBC languages section has become extremely popular.
This popularity is due both to the much larger amount of 'real' up-
to-date language material, particularly in recorded form, available
relatively cheaply, and to the fact that these courses have contributed to discussion of a nationally acceptable framework and definition of levels for adult classes.

There was a certain resistance to the new multi-media courses early
on. 'You can't possibly do all that in one lesson'. What teachers
did not always realise was that the material was there to be used in

a variety of ways. The units are, in fact, designed primarily for learners to work with at home, and the teacher working with a class is able to pick and choose what he finds useful. It is not necessary to 'do' the whole chapter before going on to the next, and a large amount of the material can be offered for homework or used for listening work only.

There is a large variety of other courses on the market for language learners, and a number of them are suitable for adults. Many of these books do have a structure which is likely to appeal to the methodically organised adult and many have very useful suggestions for imaginitive classroom activities, but there is often a serious lack of material for listening practice and of real examples of the language in use. Thus the BBC's output of multi—media courses does. at the moment have advantages, if only for the large amount of 'real' language material which is available via radio and television broadcasts at a cost which is incomparably cheaper to the learner than any other possibility.

Having chosen your course material, or perhaps having decided to prepare a course yourself from a variety of sources, it is most important that the teaching programme retains a flexible element depending on the developing needs of the students attending the class. You are not 'doing a course' with them, you are using a course to help them learn a language. What is needed from a course is a variety of authentic language material and examples of use in an attractive format and with a reasonable structure. The way things are done will vary with each teacher and each group. (Suggestions as to how a syllabus may be presented are contained in Chapter 5.)

METHODS

As you have seen from a previous chapter, language teaching has been the subject of a bewildering variety of theories. The abundance of theories on how best to help a group of people learn a language has been somewhat tempered in adult education work in this country by practical realities and the obvious need to keep the numbers in the class up. We are helped by the fact that, in general, members of our groups have the same native language and are capable of giving us mature feedback on their progress, and the philosophy which presently is most popular amongst adult education tutors could be summed up as 'if it works, use it!' The technical term for this is eclecticism - borrowing freely from a variety of sources. There is clearly much that we can use from earlier and current theories on how to teach a language. What we find most effective is to choose those techniques and approaches that suit our groups, our own personalities, the particular teaching point, the material and time available, and even the layout of the room.

There is a standard format for lesson planning for a two hour or one and a half hour adult education session which is fairly generally accepted as a basis for our work with beginners and intermediate groups:

(1) The warm up, consisting of a quick revision of previous work;

(2) Presentation of new material;

(3) Practice of the new material, with appropriate activities.

This obviously can only be a guide. Each new area of language taught may require a different approach depending on the difficulty of the concepts and vocabulary involved, the amount, type and quality of. taped and visual material available, and the inclination of the teacher and the group.

In many lessons the pattern will be merged and broken up with some items being practised before other new items are presented, and if we stick to our previous assertion that the most important factor is for people to be able to listen and understand, it is important for us to maintain this emphasis for a large part of the lesson.

In general, adult groups are likely to want to proceed to the practice and production stages immediately and will become frustrated if too much time is spent on presentation. The reasons for this are quite practical. The people are learning the language in order to be able to use it. The motivation is increased if they are able to do this from early on. Also some students may be tired from a day's work, and a lesson based on a variety of involvement and activity is more likely to give them the stimulus and break from routine that they need.

As well as ideas for presentation and practice activities, this section will consider the use of taped material, the place of reading and writing, the importance of homework, and the inclusion of additional interest material in the lesson.

(1) THE WARM UP

It is important that your lessons should start on time even if everyone is not there. If people know that you are going to wait five minutes for late-comers to drift in then they will all tend to arrive five minutes late. The late-comers will then start aiming for ten past the hour, and before you know what has happened your lesson will have drifted toward a 7.15 start instead of 7.00.

You will find it useful and probably invaluable to be in the class-room well before the lesson starts. This will give you a chance to prepare board work, arrange furniture, set up equipment and start taking the register or talking to early arrivals. It may also be possible to hold a regular short problem session for students who can come a little before the lesson begins. This is an excellent opportunity to have a tape recording of some music with words in the language you are teaching to set the atmosphere for the class.

It is then a good idea to spend the first few minutes of the lesson going over material from previous sessions. You may perhaps re-use visuals that you used last week or the week before, or use memory games such as:

Student 1   'I went to the market and bought some ham.'
Student 2   'I went to the market and bought some ham and a.
             kilo of tomatoes.'
Student 3   Adds another item, etc.

If the group knows that the lesson is likely to start with a lively warm-up of this nature they are likely to get used to adjusting their mood accordingly and a lively tempo will be set right from the start of your sessions. It is also possible that you will have fewer people coming late because they will not want to miss such a re-vision session. On the other hand it is useful also if this first five minutes or so is not essential to the whole of the lesson, because you will invariably have late-comers, and this will mean that they will not miss the presentation sessions.

Dealing with late-comers will, of course, vary depending on the personality of the teacher and the person who comes late. If the group has already developed a satisfactory atmosphere and sense of fun you might decide to take advantage of an extrovert late arrival, possibly quizzing him or her on what has caused the delay. If, however, the person is fairly sensitive you will probably decide not to, but simply welcome him or her, say what you are doing and carry on.

(2) PRESENTATION

The way that new material for a language class is presented is like-ly to vary considerably depending on the group, the teacher, the new material, the time and resources available. However, several basic principles are useful:

1) It is a good idea for the group to know that you are presenting something new so that they can concentrate their attention and know what it is! To hide this in the guide of 'natural' method is imprac-tical if you only have one or two sessions a week. Your students are studying the language in a classroom, not acquiring it like children living in the foreign country.

2) It is important to introduce new material in small stages and to try to present the group with only one difficulty at a time. For example, if you are teaching a new past tense, choose verbs that the group already know, and situations they are familiar with so that you do not include too many new nouns, for example.

3) It is useful to maintain a lively pace.

4) If you decide to use visual aids such as pictures from magazines or drawings on the board, the meaning of these should be clear.

5) Not all presentations have to be oral. A presentation to give students the vocabulary they need in order to listen to radio news might consist of their going through newspapers or a simple text to find vocabulary referring to particular themes.

6) As groups progress there will be less time spent on direct presentation and more on practice and use.

7) Your students will be keen to progress to practice activities as soon as they can. In fact, it is often a very useful device to break up long presentations with practice sessions. For example, in the presentation of the past tense in French your first verb might be **boire**. The suggestion here is not that this verb should necessarily be the first introduction to the perfect tense - if it fits with your syllabus there is, however, no reason why it should not be, and it will provide us here with an example which can be discussed.

You might start with a character on the board and draw cartoons:

Voici Georges

Ce matin il a bu un café à 8 heures

A 10 heures il a bu un chocolat

A 12 heures il a bu un demi

A 4 heures il a bu une tasse
de thé

A 7 heures il a bu un pastis

Avec son repas du soir il a bu
3 verres de vin rouge

The drawings can be done quickly, either on the board as you are
working (it is surprisingly easy to develop this 'art'), or if you
doubt your artistic ability drawings can be prepared in advance in
felt pen on card, or on an OHP transparency.

Having told the group that you are going to introduce the past
tense, your warm-up session might well concentrate on revision of
the time of day. Assuming your students are already familiar with a
variety of drinks, having perhaps learnt how to order in a café, the
only difficulty you are introducing is, therefore, the actual past
tense form <u>il a bu</u>. This is a useful starter for the new tense and
you can have a lively session of choral and individual repetition.
The pronunciation of the 'u' sound is quite memorable for the group
and is likely to stay in the mind.

It is quite clear, therefore, that you will not have to spend very
long on straightforward presentation. In fact, this might consist
quite simply of you saying what happened, i.e. reading the text, and
the students listening and understanding.

You can then go straight into practice by putting alternatives and
yes/no questions to students, e.g.

<u>Il a bu un whisky ce matin ou un thé?</u>
<u>Un thé.</u>
<u>Il a bu un thé.</u>

<u>Il a bu un café?</u>
<u>Non.</u>
<u>Non.</u> <u>Un thé.</u>
<u>Non.</u> <u>Il a bu un thé.</u>

Il a bu trois ou quatre verres de vin
avec son repas du soir?
Trois verres.
Il a bu trois verres.
Il en a bu trois.

You will see that the questions used above allow students to give short and natural sounding answers if they wish to. It is another example of the point made above that students will be able to understand more than they can actually say. The questions I have chosen require a short easy answer and put the emphasis on understanding, though more complex answers can be given. They are also a much safer type of question at this stage of the presentation. If you ask 'Qu'est-ce qu'il a fait à 8 heures?' the group not only have to understand a new form 'fait', but give an answer which is longer and which they have not just heard in the question.

When the first presentation stage is over, you need to decide whether to go straight on to a range of other verbs or whether to use other subjects. This particular example lends itself to both. You might go back to Georges' day and start talking about what he has eaten, or you might go to the group and ask them what they have drunk. The second alternative is perhaps most useful for several reasons:

- It gives the people a chance to become active more quickly and you can lead on very easily to group activities with people finding out what the others have had to drink.

- You avoid the question, for the moment, of the variety of verb forms in the perfect tense, if you wish to.

- People will be able to draw on their own experience at once. A chance for the use of imagination and humour.

- In any case, it is necessary to give ample practice of the use of the past tense when talking about oneself.

An important point about presentations of new material is that it is most unusual for what you are presenting to be 'new' to everyone in the group. In the example chosen, some of the people will have remembered 'bu' from their schooldays and others will, in any case, have read ahead in the book or listened to the record at home and will know what is coming. They are coming to your class to practise and will want to get on with this as soon as possible.

Another factor is that there will certainly be in the group a number of people who once having understood the structure 'il a bu un café au lait' will respond very well to being given a list of other past participles and examples of their use. If there are people in your group with good memories and an analytical approach it is an advantage to give them as much material as they can take even though they might get into some trouble with pronunciation.

An alternative method of continuing this presentation might be to allow the group to listen to French people talking about what they have drunk today and retain the detail, although this could already again really be said to be practice. Also, if you have a group of people who would like a list of past participles you might decide to play them a tape of conversations from the course book, and ask them how many past participles they can isolate and identify. They could check their answers against the text in the book, and you could then go through the list on the board. You could, of course, choose other verbs and give them a similarly intensive treatment to the work already done with 'boire'.

You must decide at this stage your policy on the use of technical grammatical terms, such as 'past participle'. The argument that such terms will be known by less than 10% of the population and should, therefore, not be used in class is well known. It is up to the teacher to decide what terminology he can easily simplify for the benefit of students. In this case, the question could easily be 'how many verbs can you find in the passage that refer to the past'. If you think that any member of the group does not understand the term 'verb', then tell the class what a verb is and give examples, but don't bother to do this unless there is a problem.

The second area of controversy that needs exploration in this section is that of questioning techniques. With a group in a semi-circle there is a temptation to ask questions in order round the circle so that no-one is left out. Obviously if you do this people can switch off as soon as their turn is past. They are also likely to get a crisis of nerves just as their turn is going to come. Also if you call out a name or point to a person and then ask a question, you run the same risk of putting the student too much on the spot.

The most useful technique is probably to ask the question of the whole group and then look for a person who can give an answer. Several people may call the answer out. If there is any doubt you can call on someone who got it right to repeat it. If students get to know that you only call on them to repeat if they are correct, this will boost confidence. If you get no answers you can rephrase the question or give alternatives for people to choose.

One disadvantage of the system is that you may get too many responses all at once and not be able to make them out clearly. This is not very likely with the short responses we are advocating, but in any case you can soon get over this by asking a section of the class at a time. A second possible disadvantage is that some people may not participate at all. If this happens you have to decide whether (a) this is because they are shy and prefer not to, in which case they will be able to cope when you split them into groups later, or (b) because they don't understand, in which case you will have to try to find out what the problem is without making an example of them to the rest of the group.

Difficulties over questioning techniques usually disappear as a relaxed atmosphere develops in your group and as members get to know each other. Perhaps the most important point here is that all questions asked in the early stages of language learning should be easy - either yes/no questions or alternatives, easy one-word answers, or answers that are somewhere in the question.

This general technique for questioning gives a good basis for the establishment of a lively pace in the classroom with a large degree of participation, and can, of course, be varied either by asking people to ask each other questions across the room, or by asking questions directly of people from time to time, and so on.

To sum up this section, presentation is critical in the language learning process. It is important that you make sure the steps are not too great, that the message is clear, that the class maintains a lively pace and moves quickly to use of the language being practised. Care should be taken over the use of grammatical terminology and questioning technique. Most groups of adults will want to practise the material as soon as possible and the main aim of your presentation sessions can really be said to enable students to move rapidly to using language with understanding.

(3) PRACTICE

The reasons why you want to get on with practical work are several:

-   The group is learning the language in order to be able to use it. Students need practice of the language in use;

-   If the students see an immediate practical application of what they are learning, this is likely to increase motivation;

-   In any case, a group of adults, some probably tired after work, is likely to respond well to a teaching method that gives a chance to be active for a large part of the lesson.

It is clear that in order to be able to use a lot of activities in the class, the group you are working with must be aware of what you are hoping to achieve and must be prepared to accept the 'rules of the game' from time to time. Most adults will enter into such a contract with enthusiasm if they understand the purpose fully and it is worth having a discussion about the approach in English at some stage fairly early on in the course.

In this section I shall give examples of different types of activities that can be used effectively with groups of adult learners at various stages of language learning. They are only examples but from them some general principles emerge. The type of exercise I am choosing is that which gives the group the chance to communicate meaningfully in the language as early as possible. There is a note on the importance of accuracy in communication at the end of the section.

Memory games

Very often in beginners or near-beginners groups the tutor brings to the class a collection of objects, puts them on the table and practices the following sentences with prepositions:

'There's a cigarette on the table'
'There's a pencil next to the rubber...' etc.

Such exercises can be made very much more effective after the initial presentation by covering over the objects or putting them in a box or bag, and getting the group to try to remember what is there, possibly working in pairs or individually. Always warn them you are going to do it and impose a time limit. This game is, of course, known as Kim's game and is a children's party favourite. The point for foreign language learners is that you are giving them a task for which they have to use the foreign language.

It is a memory test, but in order to do well the brain has to get rid of any excess information and will try to work as quickly as possible. You will find that this pressure of time and information has two effects. Firstly, the students will try to abbreviate the sentences they should be using. Instead of 'There's a book in the bag', they are likely to say just 'Book'. You may perhaps correct this to 'And a book' to get the use of language as normal as possible. Secondly, and most importantly, you will find that many students stop translating and start 'thinking in the language'. This is the aim that adults always state, but it is difficult to know when students start to reach it. This type of exercise is a clear example of pressure on the short-term memory forcing the brain to economise and avoid the slower processes of translation.

Variations of this technique can, of course, be used with other material - picture stories, description of a scene or people, tabulated information, such as a diary for the week or a list of opening times. The material can vary according to the items of language being practised but the basic principle is the same - the group is given a short time to memorise the information - not too

73

little or too much - and then pools its resources to remember as much as possible.

The overhead projector is useful for such exercises in that an image can easily be presented, covered up and then presented again, but obviously pictures, drawings and the blackboard can also be used effectively.

A variation on this principle, which allows for intensive practice of listening skills, is for the tutor to read a short statement or description and then give a second alternative with one or two small changes. Again the short term memory is put under pressure in the foreign language, the brain needs to economise in order to store all the necessary information and therefore avoids the temptation to translate. Here is an example of this for near beginners in French, read quickly by the teacher:

Tutor: What's different in the second sentence?
Pierre aime le théâtre, le cinéma mais déteste tous les sports.
Pierre aime le théâtre, le cinéma et les livres mais déteste tous les sports.
Students: Il aime les livres.

Obviously such material must be well prepared in advance, but once this has been done the tutor can keep a sheet of quick oral exercises for each point covered for revision purposes or re-use with other groups.

Surveys

A useful way of putting the students in a position where they are able to use the language early on, which can be applied to many different teaching points is the mock survey. In the previous section's example of teaching the past tense of boire, you might start after demonstrating vous avez bu by asking students to find out what their neighbour has had to drink over some time this week.

A condition is that the question form Qu'est-ce que vous avez bu? may not be used. Answers must be 'yes' or 'no'. Assuming the group already knows the necessary drinks vocabulary and can cope reasonably enough with the partative structure du, de la, des, the conversations might go like this:

Vous avez bu du whisky?
Non.
Vous avez bu de la bière?
Oui.
Un verre?
Non.

Deux verres?
Oui.
Vous avez bu du cognac?
Oui.
Un verre?
Oui
Vous avez bu d'autres boissons? etc

If they do this, it will be clear that by practising the tense in
such a way early on the students are already thinking in the past
and leaving out the verb in supplementary questions, which is, of
course, a lot easier and what French people would do in real speech.
For this particular activity a demonstration tape would obviously be
most useful for the beginning of the session.

From this particular example and from others it is clear that by
using these techniques you can be sure that your students will
actually get lots of practice in asking questions, which is essential if they are going to function properly abroad, and not a common
teaching point with more traditional approaches.

Card matching activities

The previous example depended on the use of the personal experience
of the learners and could of course have led to confusion if they
had had too many different sorts of drinks and did not know the
necessary vocabulary. A way of limiting the vocabulary in use and,
therefore, reducing the risk of confusion is to provide information
on prepared cards. One such possibility would be in talking about
likes and dislikes. Prepare a set of cards like this:

Vous aimez	Vous n'aimez pas
le rugby	la télévision
le cinéma	les supermarchés
aller à la....	fumer
la bière anglaise	la bière française
le théâtre	manger au restaurant
le thé anglais	

Make a set of sixteen cards in which there are eight matching pairs.
The cards are distributed at random and the students are asked to
find people in the group who have similar likes and dislikes to
them. Such an activity which encourages students to move around the
class and talk to others may, of course, necessitate a more flexible
seating arrangement. The important point here is that there is a
real opportunity for communication to take place, because there is
an information gap to fill. This information gap between two or more
people is fundamental to the idea of real communication. There is
not much purpose in asking someone about something you already know.
Activities which use an information gap may be made up quite easily

and organised with the use of cue cards. An example is given here, in which people enquire about train times. One student has the Cue Card A and the other has the Cue Card B - one asks for information, the other gives it. The student with Cue Card A notes down the answers by the other student, as one would at a railway station.

Cue Card A	Cue Card B
⟶ Bonn? Wann ab? Wann an? Umsteigen?	⟶ Bonn ab 10.34 an 12.01 U - Köln

Cue Card A	Cue Card B
⟶ Paris? Départ? Arrivée? Direct?	⟶ Paris Dép. - 10.34 Arr. - 12.01 changer à Orléans

In such tasks each student has to communicate successfully in order to complete the task.

More advanced work

These three basic techniques can be adapted for use with different verb tenses as they are introduced. Of course, as the group becomes more advanced you will probably be able to give more freedom for them to use a wider range of vocabulary. For example, by the time you are practising the conditional tense you should be able to perhaps ask the group to guess what a particular member of the group would do if he had £50,000. In order to make an activity of this you might ask the student to write down six things he would do:

'I would go on a world trip', 'I would buy a new car', etc, choosing from a list of say twelve possibilities prepared by you. The rest of the group then work in pairs or small groups trying to decide which choices that particular student has made.

By using a variety of situations students can be brought to solve quite complicated problems with the aid of a few cues on card. For example:

76

A police investigation of an accident or crime;
Asking a person about their holidays;
Explaining an injury or illness to the doctor;
Explaining you have lost something and describing the object.

In each of these cases it is possible to give cues to students or to give them roles to play.

PRACTISING A FUNCTION

Talking about yourself and your family and asking this of others

This is a particularly useful activity for the beginning of an intermediate course or perhaps a short residential course or day school, as it gives people a good opportunity to get to know each other. Give the students a questionnaire sheet about themselves with, for French, the following headings:

Nom   Travail
Age (voluntary)   Famille
Domicile   Intérêts
Maison

Ask them to complete the detail. Then collect in papers, number them, tear off the names and perhaps the ages and pin them around the wall. It is then the task of the students to find the number of everyone in the group. There are obvious possibilities of confusion and inaccuracy in this activity but it gives a far more memorable start to a course than the more traditional approach of the teacher at the front of the class asking questions of everyone in turn. As groups are more advanced obviously the scope of the questionnaire can be enlarged.

Finding the way

This is a very common topic in courses for travellers and beginners in a language, and there are many activities that can be organised around it. Remember that the students are going to need to ask the questions and understand the answer.

1) Using a simple town plan ask the class to follow your directions and then tell you where they are. The dialogue might go like this:
'Vous sortez de la gare. Vous tournez à droite. Vous continuez 200 mètres. Qu'est-ce que vous avez sur votre droite? Un super-marché? Oui. Vous tournez à gauche dans le passage, et vous avez une banque sur votre droite ou votre gauche? Sur votre droite, oui...'

When this has been practised for a while and students have a reasonable grasp of the words and structures, they can be asked to do it in a simpler way in pairs or small groups with one student giving directions and the others following the route.

2) Give the students a blank piece of paper (or for a simpler exercise, one with a few streets marked on it), and ask them to draw a plan which you dictate to them. When this has been practised it can again be done in small groups. Alternatively, produce two maps of the same town, one having more detail than the other. Students have to work in pairs, not looking at each other's maps, and each trying to find out what is missing from his or her map. This again is the principle of the 'information gap'. The student's task is actually to find something out from another student who knows it.

3) When the group is quite proficient at giving and receiving directions you might organise a 'Treasure Trail' around the building with prepared clues either on a sheet or pinned up en route. There may, of course, be the condition which applies to all these activities that, once started, the use of English is banned.

Practising with pictures

Pictures are traditionally used for presenting new language material, in which case they should be large and clear, and used from the front of the class. It is also extremely effective to use pictures and cartoons for small group practice and pair work.

- Ordering a sequence. Groups are given a set of picture cards and asked to put them in order. Pictures showing a series of actions, or events in a person's day are possibilities. The students have to prepare a commentary in the foreign language.

- What's the difference? Pictures with small differences give a stimulus to speak and are particularly useful for pair work practice of negative constructions: Il y a un bouteille de lait sur le premier dessin mais il n'y a pas de bouteille de lait sur le deuxième or Il n'y en a pas sur le deuxième or Sur le deuxième dessin il n'y a pas de bouteille de lait.

- Choosing the picture to fit the description. Prepare a collection of fairly similar magazine pictures and captions. The captions are read out and members of the group have to find the appropriate picture.

- Information transfer. Students describe pictures or cartoons to each other so that they can be drawn. They then compare the originals with the reproductions. A useful topic here is 'Identikits'. If your group has been learning the language needed for describing people, it is possible to organise very effective pair work by getting some cartoons of different people, copying them and cutting up one of the copies into an identikit jigsaw. One student is given the original cartoon, the other is given a selection of jigsaw features from which to choose, using his partner's instructions to make up a face. Obviously for such an exercise, the necessary vocabulary and questions forms must be very carefully prepared, but the activity is so effective it is well worth the necessary preparation.

- Guessing. Certain pictures may lend themselves to guessing activities. One excellent example is a group photo of people of some twelve different nationalities. The group are asked to guess who is who. Pictures and hidden objects may be used extremely effectively for 'Twenty Questions' games. For example, a student is given a picture of a personality, and the rest of the group have to guess who it is. Only yes/no answers are allowed.

- Shopping. In pairs, one student acts as the shopkeeper and the other as the customer. The customer knows what is for sale, but does not know the prices. He or she is given a set amount of money, say 100F, and the task is to get the best possible value for this.

- Train timetables. Working in pairs or small groups one student is given route maps for public services between two towns. Another student is given the appropriate timetable. The timetables have been worked out in such a way that it is better to travel different ways at different times of day. The student with the map has to work out how to travel from A to B leaving at different times. He or she needs to get the necessary timetable information from the other student, who in turn has to work out the language needed from the timetable and various timetable symbols. Students must not, of course, look at each other's papers.

The following exercise of this type has been translated from an EFL (English as a foreign language) exercise. Progress in methodology in EFL has been more rapid than in the teaching of modern languages in this country, and can provide many stimulating ideas for language teachers. The exercise:

Student A. You wish to travel from Chalanges to Rézanne, to arrive before 12.30 pm. As you will see from the map there is a choice of bus and rail services. Find out from Student B the most suitable route and make an note of the times and details.

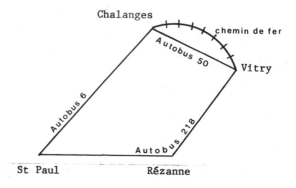

Chalanges

chemin de fer

Autobus 50

Vitry

Autobus 6

Autobus 218

St Paul

Autobus

Rézanne

Student B You will be asked about the best way to travel between Chalanges and Rézanne. You have the following information:

<table>
<tr><td>

Autobus Ligne 6
Chalanges - St. Paul
Départ
    07.55
    08.55
et ainsi de suite
jusqu'à
    21.55
Durée du voyage -
    1h. 10m.

</td><td>

Trains
Chalanges - Vitry
    07.10
    08.10
et ainsi en suite.

Durée du voyage 1h.

A Vitry la Gare Routière
se trouve à 15 minutes à
pied de la Gare SNCF

</td></tr>
</table>

Autobus Ligne 50
Chalanges - Vitry

Chalanges	9.10	12.10	16.40	21.00
Vitry	10.15	13.15	17.45	22.00

Autobus Ligne 218
Vitry - St. Paul

Vitry	9.10	10.10	et ainsi	21.10
Rézanne	9.50	10.50	de	20.50
St. Paul	10.05	11.05	suite	21.05
			jusqu'à	

St. Paul	10.10	11.10	12.10
Rézanne	10.25	11.25	12.25
Vitry	11.05	12.05	13.05

Larger Simulations

Most of the activities listed above can be fitted into short slots in the lesson to give the necessary practice at appropriate times at a fairly lively and varied pace. It is also possible to devise simulations that give groups a real chance for extended practice of the language.

- **Une semaine de Paris.** This simulation assumes that the group has had thorough practice of the structures and vocabulary involved in inviting people out, and has had a chance to listen to and imitate examples of French people doing this. You need a number of maps of Paris, a duplicated diary for the students, and a selection from the Paris 'What's on' guide, <u>Une semaine de Paris</u>. Ask the students to decide where they are staying and to check with the map and guide to decide where they would like to go during their stay. The task is then for them to make arrangements to go to places they would like to visit, making a new arrangement each day with a different person in the group. English is obviously banned, and it also helps if the students do not write arrangements in their diaries until their conversations are completed.

The arrangements should include times and places of meeting, means of transport, cost, what to do afterwards, etc, and the language used can become quite involved and certainly very genuine. The simulation can take some time and can, of course, be stopped if time runs out or when you notice a serious mistake that needs correction. In general, however, it is a good idea to let things continue as long as interest is maintained, to give your students a good chance to complete the task. For consolidation the diary can, of course, be written up later, probably for homework.

This section also gives you several examples of games and activities which can be used to give people the chance to practise use of a language, and is by no means complete. As you gain experience in using the basic principles outlined above you will find you can invent games and activities to give intensive practice of different language items.

The need for this approach to the work with adult groups is clear. It is necessary at this stage to add a few words about accuracy. It is quite clear that encouraging your group to use the language as early as possible may well lead to a higher proportion of 'mistakes'. The students are likely to try to use words they do not know and get them wrong. This is made worse if the words 'work' and the person the student is working with understands, as they will then be reinforced as part of the learner's vocabulary. Even worse, students may begin to copy each other's mistakes.

The teacher must be listening for serious mistakes and be prepared to stop individuals or the whole group for correction and drilled practice. Students are likely to be glad of such correction and it will be accepted eagerly as it enables the learner to get on with the activity more effectively. This being said, we must remember that the mistake is not really important unless it is likely to lead to a lack of comprehension or the formation of bad habits, which are likely to get in the way of effective communication or hinder subsequent learning. While accuracy can be one of our general aims we should remember that most of our students are learning for practical rather than academic purposes, and need to get by in a variety of situations rather than excel.

Clearly some ideas advocated in this section demand some preparation time. This time decreases as you become more proficient at producing communicative exercises to suit different purposes, and, of course, each new exercise produced will be available for other groups and for next time. A further advantage is that the activities occupy students for a good period of time, and all students can be occupied in contrast to the situation in which the teacher engages the student in one-to-one conversation. It is also true to say that such active learning methods are very popular and, of course, contribute greatly to confidence and fluency.

In conclusion, it is worth mentioning that the use of activities which enable the teacher to step off the stage at the front of the class does give a chance to watch from the wings. If the group is working together on an activity or task the teacher is able to stand aside and consider how particular individuals are progressing, and notice features of the group he or she might otherwise miss. While there is probably a greater amount of preparation for such a teaching style, there is less pressure while the actual session is in progress, and considerable advantages in terms of student achievement, motivation, and use of time.

USING TAPES

We have seen that tapes of actuality material are vital for presenting and practising the language. It is also essential to spend a certain amount of time working with such taped material in order to give your group plenty of opportunities to hear the spoken word.

Even if you are a native speaker it is still advisable to use taped recordings to give your groups the opportunity to listen to different people of both sexes in different situations.

You may just ask your students to listen to a passage which has sufficient intrinsic interest to hold their attention in any case. With such a passage you may just ask them to note any unknown words.

82

It is normal practice to listen without following the text in the book, but the passages must be reasonably short for this or else your students may not be able to cope. You may decide to ask questions on the passage which may be given before or after it is played, depending on the extent of difficulty. If detailed concentration is needed you will, of course, ask the questions before playing the tape so that the students know what to listen for.

You may, perhaps, ask your students to make notes on a passage for summary, in which case it is often necessary to play the tape more than once. French teachers who have used <u>Allez France</u> will remember the interview with M. Laporte in Chapter 16: '<u>La vie à Puylaroque dans ma jeunesse était extremement calme. Il y avait peu de distractions et encore moins d'amusements</u>...' As the conversation continues M. Laporte gives several examples of life in the old days in Puylaroque and this is an ideal opportunity for summary work, students being asked to list differences between life then and now.

A further way of using the familiar tape recording for practical purposes and to concentrate students' attention on the spoken word is to play it again using the pause button to produce gaps for the group to give you the missing word. This activity encourages the development of anticipation when listening to the language – an essential skill in order to be able to cope with longer passages or conversations.

THE PLACE OF READING AND WRITING

While the main emphasis in your work will be on practical listening and speaking activities, there is still, of course, a place for reading and writing.

– <u>Reading</u> is particularly necessary in the early stages when potential travellers must be able to come to terms with street signs and instructions, and particularly when dealing with languages like Greek and Russian with unfamiliar alphabets. Useful activities are to give the group a selection of newspapers and ask what they can puzzle out, or to show photos of street signs for the same purpose. At this stage if people are due to travel abroad it is useful to give examples of any peculiarities of handwriting. I thought I had mastered the Greek script until I came to a village where the bus destinations were written up in the square on a blackboard.

– <u>Writing</u> is less important for most adult learners of a foreign language, although it has obvious value as a consolidation exercise to reinforce and give a reference for what has been learned. Students may be asked to produce written summaries and accounts after their practice activities, e.g. the diary in the Paris game quoted earlier; and if given as homework this will mean that no valuable time is wasted in class. At beginners level activities such as producing lists, perhaps of verbs or nouns to do with particular themes, are useful group activities as they encourage the sharing of knowledge. At all stages before advanced levels it should be remembered that to be able to write is not the ultimate aim, although a certain practical ability will be useful. Though, if you have students who want to write and take a pride in this, it can only help to give them encouragement.

OTHER INTEREST MATERIAL

In your lesson planning it is a good idea to take account of other interesting material that you can include to add variety and a memorable quality to the lesson.

- It may be possible for you to arrange visits from other native speakers to meet the group, particularly perhaps foreign language assistants who may be glad to gain different experience.

- If students in your group visit the country concerned it may be possible to persuade them to give a brief account in the foreign language of their visit. They may also be able to obtain taped material and items of interest to the class.

- If any of your group are in correspondence with people abroad you may perhaps be able to arrange an exchange of letters or tapes between classes.

- If you know that members of the group have a particular special interest in an aspect of the country whose language you are studying, you may be able to persuade them to give a short talk on this - but be careful to give adequate help while they are preparing this or the language is likely to be too difficult.

- You may be able to introduce songs into the classroom, particularly to highlight particular grammatical structures. For the presentation of the past tense quoted earlier, a recording of the Prévert poem 'Déjeuner du matin' would have been an ideal follow-up. For practical purposes and particularly to help the group concentrate their attention on a song without getting lost, it is useful to supply texts with words missing for them to insert. In this case it would have been the past participles, although a jumbled checklist may be useful to avoid too many spelling mistakes.

<u>Déjeuner du Matin</u>   Jacques Prévert

Il a _____ le café
Dans la tasse.
Il a _____ le lait
dans la tasse de café.

84

Il a _____ le sucre
dans le café au lait.
Avec la petite cuiller
Il a _____.
Il a _____ le café au lait.
Et il a _____ la tasse
Sans me parler.
Il a _____
une cigarette.
Il a _____ des ronds
avec la fumée
Il a _____ les cendres
dans le cendrier
sans me parler,
sans me regarder.
Il s'est levé,
il a ____
son chapeau sur sa tête.
Il a ____ son manteau de pluie
parce qu'il pleuvait
Et il est _____
Sous la pluie.
Sans une parole.
Et moi, j'ai ....
ma tête dans ma main,
et j'ai _____.

mis   tourné   allumé   mis   pris   fait   reposé
       mis   sorti   pleuré   mis   bu   mis

- Another source of additional interest in classes, particularly
if you have members who are theatrically inclined, is to arrange
for the preparation, rehearsal and production of short sketches and
theatre pieces. This is most valuable at the end of term, possibly
as preparation for the Christmas party, but if it becomes a major
activity for part of the group it is a good idea to persuade them to
do it largely out of class time in order not to inhibit non-actors
during the classes.

- Video, film, slides and filmstrips can provide useful interest
material in the lesson, particularly if there is specialist material
available that is particularly relevant to your course. Beware of
using too much technology in class, however. Most of your students
will have a television at home, and probably come to the class for
human contact and help with learning that they cannot get when
working alone.

When planning lessons you need to consider the place of homework. The practical difficulty here is that some members of your group will have a large part of the week to put towards learning the language, while others will have very little spare time. It is a good idea, except on very special occasions, to make homework optional in consideration of some people who just won't have time to do it. On the other hand, you should be able to give those with plenty of opportunity ideas about how to reinforce their learning out of class. It may be possible to form a syndicate to hand around taped material. A very large proportion of families has access to a basic cassette recorder. You may be able to make useful suggestions about readers or foreign radio. If you have students who really do have a lot of time to spend out of class then it may be a good idea to try to put them in touch with a foreign national who would perhaps meet them on a weekly basis, or put them in touch with the nearest facility for them to do individual language laboratory work.

One fear that does sometimes hinder this approach is that when students develop at different speeds they are likely to leave your class behind. On the other hand, it is probably likely that if you do not give people the opportunity to develop at their own speed they may leave through frustration.

CONCLUSION

From time to time many frustrations are expressed by adult education tutors. You may well be teaching in a room that is not your own, but used for other subjects and probably for school children during the day. You may not be sure that the cassette recorder will always be working, or indeed that it will even be where you left it last week. You may not be able to decorate the room as you would wish or even arrange the furniture to suit your group. If your group meets just once a week there may be problems of retention of the language, particularly if students are absent. You may find that the traditional adult education holidays give a much longer gap than your students want in the middle of a course.

You will probably find that you are under pressure to keep large numbers in your group in order to keep the group next term, and you may feel isolated in your work with little contact with other language teachers.

It is inevitable that these and other disadvantages do accrue to adult education tutors, and the next chapter shows ways in which the centre can make efforts to minimise their effect.

The advantages you have in your favour are, however, tremendous and the large number of successful languages classes around the country is witness to this. You are working with a popular subject, with a wealth of interesting up-to-date material. You are likely to have interesting groups of highly motivated people keen to learn in a refreshing and enjoyable atmosphere. They are also usually glad to find that they can succeed better in an adult class than they did at school. The most important factors that tip the scales in your favour are enthusiasm for the subject and concern for the success of your students.

REFERENCES

(1) Baer, E (ed): Teaching languages: ideas and guidance for teachers working with adults. BBC, 1976.

FURTHER READING

Brumfit, C and K Johnson (eds): The communicative approach to language teaching. Oxford University Press, 1979.

Krashen, S D: Principles and practice in second language acquisition Pergamon Press, 1982.

Littlewood, W T: Communicative language teaching. Cambridge University Press, 1981.

Wilkins, D A: Notional syllabuses. Oxford University Press, 1976.

THE TUTOR, THE HEAD OF CENTRE AND IN-SERVICE EDUCATION

Duncan Sidwell

The organisation of evening and day courses for adults and the provision of in-service education for tutors are closely connected. In adult education where the absence of strong formal structures is so evident there is a particular need for those who are involved to provide mutual help and support. The lack of formal structures and the fact that part-time and permanent staff do not see each other all that frequently mean that very positive steps need to be taken by all within the service to make it work well. Greater awareness of the need for mutual support, for support structures and the engendering of a feeling of professionalism among tutors can only help a service which is having to struggle in many ways. It is, therefore, worthwhile considering the relationships and obligations which the different parts of the service have to each other, what the contribution of members of that service should be and what may be done in the way of in-service education. This chapter is, therefore, divided into two sections. In the first part the roles of the tutor, the head of centre and what may be done in any particular area are considered. In the second part the in-service education of tutors is discussed.

PART 1: THE TUTOR, THE HEAD OF CENTRE AND THE LOCAL AREA

The 'cellular' nature of adult education can easily lead to lack of awareness among those who contribute to it of how extensive the activity is. This may be hidden particularly from individual tutors, whose contacts can be restricted to one class and to a head of centre. Teaching in these circumstances may make it difficult to realise that one is part of a very significant element in the life of many adults in our community. Some two million adults each year are involved in classes of some sort (1), and languages are a significant part of this provision. In Leicestershire, for example, in the years 1978/79 the number of adult students of foreign languages actually outnumbered the students in schools who took 'O' and 'A' level language examinations. The fact that most adult students (some 60%) (2) will attend a language course for one year only, indicates the extensive and constantly renewed pool of demand which exists. To teach all these students within the one county there are some 150 tutors — a considerable fund of professional knowledge and expertise. In spite of the extensive nature of the enterprise and the very clear social demands of this provision, the view persists in some quarters that adult education is not terribly important, is amusement, or at least, is not entirely serious. To an extent this has coloured the self-image of those working in the sector as a whole, as well as the degree of provision of funds and of in-service education. The 1944 Education Act certainly intended that adult education should be a charge on public funds, but the view that adult education is not vital for the health of the community is reflected in the resources which are made available to it in many parts of the country. Yet there are at least three reasons why it is important. Clearly, a well-organised and efficiently professional service is of great value to the health of the community in terms of the companionship, exchange of opinion and the pursuit of interest and personal development which it facilitates. It provides important outlets and opportunities for many people and, as such, has a place in our social fabric which is not supplied by other agencies. This general function is, in fact, acknowledged in the 1944 Act where in Section 7 (iii) the duty is laid on each Local Authority to 'contribute towards the spiritual, moral, mental and physical development of the community by securing that efficient education throughout those stages (i.e.primary, secondary and further) shall be available to meet the needs of the population of their area.'

The second reason why an efficiently run service is important is that it is an opinion-former relating to the quality of the education service in general. A well-run adult education centre with professionally minded tutors providing good courses will increase confidence in the service. It must be remembered that some of the adult students may not have all that favourable a view of schools and education to begin with, and the quality of the provision they encounter will counteract or confirm this view - and of course, influence their view of the education of their children and grandchildren.

There is also a third and fundamentally important aspect of adult education: it provides a whole area of voluntary educational activity whose influence on our view of how education in school should be conducted is not inconsiderable. It provides in some senses an alternative view of education and its purposes, or at least, a major additional perspective. This exploration of the purpose and nature of education is significant, and adult education's influence on the education of young people should not be under-estimated. In fact, in the field of modern languages a concrete example of this influence is provided by the work of the Council of Europe group of experts in languages in adult education. This group, led by John Trim, has worked out new analyses of language in terms of functions. These have had a major influence on school language teaching. It was, in part, the stimulus and lead given by this work in the adult field which led to the growth of the graded assessment movement in modern languages in our schools and to a reappraisal of the objectives of school language teaching. In adult education there has been room for experiment and development which schools, dominated by old-fashioned and inappropriate examinations, have found, and continue to find, difficult to achieve.

There are many ways in which the adult education system provides a healthy check and reference point for the period of statutory schooling. This is not the place to go into the question of why young people are in school or what they should be doing whilst there. Suffice it to say it is not self evident. Adult education, which of its nature tends to be continuing education, offers us a perspective of education as a continuing process of experience, rather than as a preparation of the next stage, or preparation for life. Adult education is also able to change and respond quickly to demand — something the school system is not able to do easily because of the examination system and the political pressures which exist concerning the content of the curriculum. Adult education is relatively free of these pressures, and its existence as a voluntary and hence, seminal element within the education system as a whole should not go unrecognised. The adult education world is in some ways a test bed of education as process rather than as result, and those tutors and permanent staff who specialise in this field have much to give to education in general in a society just into the post-mechanical industrial era.

THE TUTOR AND THE ORGANISATION OF COURSES

In an earlier chapter in this volume David Smith looked at the differences between school children and adults as learners. It may be useful here to consider some of the differences and similarities which exist in terms of organisation of courses and the level of training of teachers in schools and of tutors in adult education.

In seeking ways of responding to demand adult education cannot look towards the school model for a variety of reasons. Although the experience of many tutors and some full-time staff will have been within the school — all of them certainly as students — this experience does not necessarily provide guidance as to how classes should be run or organised for adults. Yet, if we do look at some aspects of the organisation of courses for adults in the light of the organisation of classes in school, then it becomes apparent that there are some clear deficiencies in adult education provision:

—   We assume that a native speaker of English in our schools needs some form of subject-specific training in order to teach English, yet we find in adult classes that native speakers of a foreign language often have to learn how to teach without help or guidance, and frequently without any formal language education prior to entering the classroom.

—   It is taken as self-evident that a school-teacher should have spent some time during a training period and through in-service education, thinking about the nature of childhood, adolescence and so on; yet we accept without much surprise the possibility of teachers of adults somehow knowing about adulthood and its various stages, about how adults learn and about how they may best be helped to attain their goals.

- In schools, language learning is sequential. One year leads to the next and commonly one course is used throughout a three- or five-year course of study. In adult education it is unfortunately relatively rare to find sequential learning over a period of years.

- The school child is taught by a teacher who is usually a member of a team or a department, the members of which see each other regularly, and in many cases, have structured meetings. The adult language tutor is more likely than not an individual who teaches a class without reference to any other teacher, and it appears to be the exception rather than the rule that meetings of tutors take place.

- Adult students buy a course of language learning and abandon it whenever they like; this is not the case for school children.

- There is almost an industry which has grown up around school language learning. Many courses exist, publishers are responsive to demand, and although there is not necessarily agreement on its nature, there is a well-established modern languages examination system catering for about a third of all school students aged sixteen. The contrast with adult education is clear - only in recent years have courses increased in number and there are no examination goals made available to most students. The BBC courses, some of which have examinations linked to them, are actually designed for the home learner - not for the class. This is a great pity really, and somewhat incomprehensible, as clearly more people attend classes than learn languages at home and the drop-out rate among home learners is at least three times that of class attenders. (3,4) Paradoxically, however, the foreign language needs of adults are more easily predicted than those of the child at school, and it is also clear which skills need emphasising. We would consider that a school failed in its duty if it did not offer the possibility to take examinations, and yet the examinations which do exist for the adult learner are not widely on offer to him or her because of the lack of centres and perhaps because of the lack of awareness of these examinations among tutors. All too often the inappropriate GCE 'O' level examination is offered to adults as a goal.

Perhaps when seen in this contrasting light some of the needs, both in organisation and training, become more apparent. We have seen that the success of adult education depends to a great extent on the successful interlocking of various elements in the total organisation. These interlocking parts include the tutor's relationship to the centre where he or she works, the effectiveness of the head of centre, the centre's relationship to other centres and to the LEA's adult education administration and advisory services. As the point at which this organisation first touches the student is at the point of sale, then it is here that we should begin looking at what is required in terms of organisation and responsibility for it.

THE TUTOR AND THE PRESENTATION OF COURSES

There are, of course, a number of things for which a tutor is responsible. First among these is good quality teaching and a number of chapters in this volume discuss that question. The tutor also, however, has an important administrative role connected with publicity, and it is this particular aspect of the tutor's job which will be discussed here. The drafting of detailed publicity for a course is the responsibility of the person who will teach it in consultation with his or her colleagues. This publicity is clearly important, and in order to avoid wasting the prospective students' time the details should provide as clear a specification as possible. There is sometimes a conflict of interest here. Small centres, in their desire to put on a language class may be tempted to be all things to all people and create classes where the range of experience and knowledge of the language is too wide. This, while understandable, leads very often to frustration and drop-out. There is evidence that people in search of a language course - at least those who form the bulk of the attending age group - will travel some distance to find a class which suits them (2), and there seems no reason why they should not be helped in their search by being provided with adequate information about the length, content and nature of courses available at centres within travelling distance, so that they can make a reasonable choice.

It is helpful to think in terms of a contract here. Too often the student buys a course of lessons which is unspecified in content and which he or she accepts on trust. Language tutors can, and should be encouraged to be specific about the content of the course in terms of what the learner will actually achieve. The course content may seem self-evident to the tutor, but there is absolutely no reason to suppose that twenty different adults will have the same perspective. Hence the need for a detailed statement. It is probably best for course publicity to be done in two stages and at two levels of detail:

a) A general statement about the type of course giving dates, times, fees, etc and the learning elements which will be included; a note about materials which the student may have to buy; the place of the course in an overall scheme, if such exists, e.g. examination possibilities and continuation courses.

b) A detailed statement giving the course outline over a period of weeks; the materials required. This sould be available on and before the enrolment period.

This publicity should be worked out in conjunction with the head of centre not just from the point of view of its timing and general organisation, but so that the head of centre is informed about what is going on, can provide for needs and can answer queries which may come to him or her.

How can a tutor help a prospective student make the right choice?

Remembering that the prospective student will probably have his or her school experience in mind and that this experience may be different from what he or she wants now, the publicity must be explicit about what will be learned. What the adult learner will want to know is, 'What will I be able to do at the end of the course?' A course in car maintenance will equip a person to cope with specified minor repairs after say twenty weeks; a maths course will teach specific operations; a course in design will enable one to go home with something one has made, or one will have learnt several useful techniques to apply. The specification for a foreign language course should give an indication of exactly what it is intended to cover, not in terms of grammar, but in terms of situations one finds oneself in when abroad or with foreign people, and of the types of things one may wish to say.

The following is an example of adequate initial publicity for one type of course (5). It tells you who the course is intended for, its length, why you may benefit, the language areas to be covered and the administrative details you will need to know as a prospective student:

- These courses should interest people who, having little or no knowledge of the language of the country they intend to visit, wish to gain sufficient knowledge of the language to cope with the situations in which they are likely to find themselves.

- The aim of the six-week courses is to provide a 'survival' knowledge of the language and the country concerned, and thus enable the intending visitor to that country to gain greater pleasure from the holiday abroad.

- The language will be strictly limited to necessities for 'survival': ordering meals; asking the way; shopping; enquiring as to the price; hotel bookings; travel; social situations.

- Relevant information on the historic cultural background of the language would also be presented in the form of slides and films.

    (The details go on to give times, fees and an address and telephone number where further information can be obtained.)

An example of a detailed specification for a longer course is given below (6). Here the tutor has specified the topics and situations which will be covered throughout the course so that it is clear to any prospective student exactly what the course will cover:

1) Arrival in country - airport, seaport, station, customs formalities. Meeting friends.
2) Taxi rides - destination, name of street, giving addresses, paying fare, tipping.
3) In the hotel - booking room, cost, details, mealtimes, etc.
4) Complaining to the hotel manager - change of room, service, etc.
5) In the restaurant - reading the menu, ordering and paying for food, eating habits, specialities, drinking habits.
6) Asking the way - bus and tram rides, paying fare, asking for destination.
7) At the bank/bureau de change.
8) Post office - buying stamps, sending telegrams, use of telephone, collecting mail.
9) Enquiries at Tourist Office - information material, tours of region, week-end excursions, planning itineraries, Sunday and special tickets, hours of opening of museums and art galleries.
10) Railway station - buying a ticket, timetable, left luggage, which platform.
11) Shops - making purchases, paying, buying presents.
12) Visiting families - introduction, description of house/ apartment, discussion of children, giving names and relationships.
13) At the police station - reporting theft/loss of possession, description of accident.
14) Car hire - driving licence, insurance, rental, choice of models, regulations.
15) At the garage - reporting faults, spares, buying petrol.
16) Visits to football matches, cinema, theatre.
17) Visit to doctor - describing minor ailments; visit to chemist - buying pharmaceutical products.
18) Guided tour of museum, cathedral, castle; relaying information in commentary in target language to a friend.
19) Departure - paying bill at hotel. Farewells to acquaintances.

How does this compare with the following specification for a one-year course?

Stage 1 (First year)

Pronunciation and introduction to French conversation and some basic grammar.

What is missing in this totally inadequate example is any indication

94

of content whatsoever. What sort of language will be used? What exactly will be pronounced? What is 'French conversation'? What do you talk about? What is 'basic grammar' to the layman, indeed, to anyone? Both the prospective student and the head of centre are entitled to know very much more about the content of a course than this example gives.

Many tutors may not issue a course description because they find it convenient to use a particular course book over a period of a year or more. This certainly does have advantages. It only has advantages for the student, however, if the content of the book corresponds to his or her needs rather than to the tutor's convenience. One of the problems here is that the adult student, whose only experience of language learning has been at school, has only that model to judge language learning by. The chances are that school experience was academic, bookish and probably not communicative – yet the child believed it was 'learning a language', even though it could possibly say little at the end of five years of study. Very often the adult student will, therefore, expect the same sort of learning, and will experience the same sort of failure – a failure that he or she is very likely to blame on him or herself rather than on the method, the book or the tutor (2). The tutor, therefore, has a real responsibility to develop a course which will correspond to the needs of the adult learner – needs which, because of relatively limited experience, the learner may well not be able to specify in any detail. To offer a course in which the learner believes he or she is learning something useful, but is, in fact, not doing so, does somewhat take advantage of the student's ignorance of what is possible.

Using a course book over a period does not, of course, prevent a tutor issuing a specification. It must, though, be accurate, and if the course book is basically one which aims to teach a grammatical progression, then this can be set out – i.e. in Lesson 1 we will learn the 'definite article'; in Lesson 2 the 'indefinite article', and so on. I am not suggesting that such a course would be desirable, attractive or useful. It would at least tell anyone contemplating a course what to expect if he or she signed up. If the course book is one which deals with language in situations, then these too can be described so that the student can make a judgement about whether to join and whether to buy the book.

If the course is advertised as conversation, it should be made quite clear what sort of things will be talked about, or what subject of discussion may be suggested to students as suitable. In all language courses there must be an element of give and take, and all examples given above should be open to some amendment in line with students' wishes.

The main point is that in a subject which is as sequential as language learning both the head of centre and the prospective student may quite reasonably expect to receive a full specification of content. The tutor should also remember that the head of centre may not be a linguist and, in order to answer queries, will need this specification. Tutors who are not asked for such course details should clearly feel no diffidence about pushing them under the nose of the head of centre!

Tutors who would like help in evolving a syllabus in French, or German and selecting material for a Level 1 course will find the productions of the adult education organisation of the Federal Republic of Germany most useful. Short books which are an analysis of language and situational language in French and German are available from:

Pädagogische Arbeitsstelle des DVV e.V., Wolfgangstrasse 68, V Stock, 6 Frankfurt-am-Main, Federal Republic of Germany.

ADVICE TO STUDENTS

We have seen how important publicity is, and it is equally important for tutors to ensure that students are properly placed on courses once they begin to arrive. Only in large centres is it possible to provide a diagnostic try-out period followed by the setting of the groups to suit the students levels, as has been done at the Rowlinson Centre in Sheffield. In smaller centres it is often a question of giving good advice, and heads of centre should encourage their tutors to be present so that they can explain what is involved in the courses. The need for this is pointed out by the comment of a drop-out, 'I was advised by a steward and not by the teacher'. This ex-student was not able to talk to the course tutor on enrolment evening, which would have been desirable and which might have prevented his dropping out. The initial personal contact with the institution has been shown time and again to be important. Any difficulties which may be felt by potential students will lead to lower participation. In terms of social class, too, this should not be ignored. It may well be that less favoured groups in society are more easily discouraged from attending language classes particularly, because of manner and initial contact. Even so apparently minor a thing as the way in which telephone calls are handled can be very significant to people who are making their first return visit to the world of the education institution. The receptionist who is well informed, who can put his or her hand on the relevant information and who puts the caller at ease is of great value.

A brief word may also be said here about the nature of publicity and enrolment. The enrolment procedure should be made as easy as possible for students, and publicity should really try to reach out. Many students read of classes in the locality bulletins which are delivered by volunteers. This has appeared in a number of surveys to be a very effective means of reaching people. Local radio, local free trade papers, good posters, information offices, libraries and so on are all channels through which to create the idea that the local centre is a place to go to.

THE HEAD OF CENTRE AND THE TUTORS

The organisation of contact with the public falls to the head of centre, and behind this lies the question of how far he or she is responsible for the curriculum of the centre. Since it is likely that the head of centre appoints the staff, then he or she tacitly assumes this responsibility - otherwise there would be little point in selecting staff for particular purposes with particular skills. This ultimate responsibility for the quality of courses offered means that the head of centre needs to know what is going on and needs to take a hand in the co-ordination of the teaching pro-grammes. This is particularly necessary as far as modern languages is concerned in those centres where more than one language is offered or where a number of tutors are responsible for the differ-ent levels in one or more language.

One of the constant complaints of tutors is that they are isolated from one another. 'I very much enjoyed the contact with fellow teachers', is a frequently heard sentiment, here expressed recently in a letter to the writer. Yet one wonders how often this desire and need is satisfied organisationally within a centre. Partly because of the lack of a structure in the payment system for tutors and partly because of the size of some centres, it is difficult to create a head of department in some areas. Yet it should be possible to convene occasional meetings at which the course content, the materials used and the nature of publicity are discussed.

The advantages to the staff of proper organisational structure are many. The first and most important advantage is that discussion of language teaching is likely to heighten the general awareness among tutors and keep them abreast of change and development. 'We meet at registration - once a year?' is an actual comment from a tutor, which shows a desire to meet colleagues, a loss of potential good will and mutual support, and a clear lack of awareness on the part of the head of centre. The trouble with the isolation of the teacher is that it tends to be self-perpetuating and self-reinforcing. The less contact one has with one's fellow teachers the less easy it is to make contact - shyness, inhibition and even suspicion can grow and build up barriers. People acknowledge each other's presence by a 'Hello, how are you?' but that is sometimes as far as it goes. Co-operation means sharing materials, ideas and experience. It means giving mutual support. Of course, the head of centre has a critical role to play here.

In meetings, questions raised by the head of centre provide useful

starting points for discussion, even though he or she may not be an
expert in languages, and they also establish the important principle
that there are others in the institution besides the individual
tutors, who have a professional interest and responsibility towards
what any one tutor does in the classroom, and that classrooms are
not islands. This is put quite clearly in the report 'Protecting the
Future for Adult Education' in which heads of centre are urged to
'pay regular advisory visits to courses and to encourage open discussion on teaching methods between teachers and students'. (1) Such
co-ordination should also bring advantages to the students. It is
useful and reassuring for them to know, for example, that there will
be a continuation course of the same nature as the one they have
enjoyed, whether the teacher is the same or not. If one returns to
the parallel with schools, it would be considered very undesirable,
in fact almost unethical for one year's course not to be co-ordinated with the next. It would also be considered very undesirable if
there were a lack of co-ordination between the members of a language
department and an attempt at a common methodology. In the larger
adult institutions with one or more classes or tutors such organisation should certainly be looked for.

STAFFING

The selection of staff is a major function of the head of centre and
here it may be necessary for advice to be sought if he or she is not
a linguist. It is true that heads of centre are not always in the
position of being able to choose from many candidates when they wish
to set up a language course. This does not mean, however, that they
should take anyone, of course, just because he or she can speak the
language in question. After all, how many native English speakers
would be capable of teaching their language proficiently to
foreigners just because they happen to be able to speak it? There
are a number of questions which the head of centre should be satisfied about before making an appointment - questions which relate
specifically to the teaching of a language. He or she will naturally
wish to assess a prospective tutor's likely general capacity as a
tutor of adults. The sort of questions relating to languages which
may be asked would include some of the following:

-   What is the candidate's level of proficiency in the foreign
language? It is of little value having teachers who are not really
fluent. In language courses the teacher has to provide the linguistic model for a great deal of the time, and must therefore be
fluent if the students are to learn to speak the language, and to
understand that language well. The tutor should also know about the
country whose language he or she is teaching, so that an up-to-date
cultural picture is conveyed.

- Has the candidate any training in the teaching of a foreign language or in the teaching of his or her mother tongue? What did this consist of? Is he or she familiar with the Council of Europe work, for example?

- What experience has the candidate had? If this experience has been with children, then differences in approach should be explored; if with adults, then a syllabus should be discussed.

- What study of language has the candidate undertaken? By this is not meant learning a language, but the process of looking at language in terms of its structure and use. Some form of analysis has to precede teaching, and tutors must be aware of what is necessary for a learner and what is not.

- What does the candidate think the students should learn? The answer to this is not, of course, just 'French' or 'German', but what the content of the course should be. Here we can refer back to the specification which offered 'conversation and some basic grammar'. If this were offered as a suitable course a head of centre would be wise to probe much deeper.

- Does the candidate have any knowledge of examinations which are available? If the prospective tutor does suggest certain examinations, then the head of centre should invite discussion as to these examinations and their content.

- What course book, if any, would the candidate like to use? It is helpful if examples of the course book are looked at and discussed.

- What contribution or ideas does the candidate have about language days, exchanges, links with local foreign language societies, etc?

In a perfect world the head of centre would only appoint teachers of experience or at least, teachers with some training. This is not possible yet, and appointments are often made of people who learn on the job. This is, of course, less than desirable, but should it occur it is the responsibility of the head of centre to give as much support as possible, and to help the tutor towards a fully professional awareness. The tutor should certainly be involved in meetings with experienced teachers - perhaps at other centres - to observe lessons and be guided by an experienced tutor. For an inexperienced and untrained teacher to be put in the position of helping others to learn is neither fair to that group of people, nor to the tutor, nor is it professionally desirable. It cannot be assumed either, that trained teachers, experienced only in working with children, will automatically adjust to teaching adults appropriately and there is evidence which suggests that many do have some difficulty. Such tutors too may value professional guidance.

So far the head of centre's role in relation to staff development and appointment has been discussed but there is also an important job to be done in the physical organisation of the department and its resources and the promotion of activities outside the actual language course.

One of the effects of having a well-led department of languages is that more ideas tend to surface. Once people have become used to sharing ideas they also tend to see more possibilities of action. We have seen how far it is desirable for there to be occasional staff meetings to discuss courses. This may only be a beginning of a much more co-ordinated provision for adults.

An example of such an integrated organisation is the Brasshouse Centre in Birmingham. At this centre language teachers meet and plan together. A common element is the use of BBC materials and this has enabled the head of centre to suggest a number of co-ordinating features which enrich the students' experience. Apart from ensuring the adequate provision of OHP's and tape recorders, etc., the head of centre has arranged for a room to be set aside in which students may listen to tapes at any time and in which resources which relate to the courses are being collected. This, of course, means that teachers are helping each other as would be normal in a well-run school department. Courses lead to examinations of the Institute of Linguists and are sequential within the centre as well as linking with other institutions, whose students can take examinations through the Brasshouse Centre. Some of these other institutions offer higher level continuation courses leading to appropriate qualifications. One can continue at such institutions having begun to study at the Brasshouse Centre. Saturday schools, weekend courses and residential visits have grown out of this co-ordinating organisation. What is crucial in this case is that the head of centre has taken a developmental view of his job and has sought to create an organisational framework within which teachers of languages may work and expand professionally.

Part of this function is to provide for the tutors material needs. This would include consultation about which rooms to use, their lay-out and equipping them. This last point is of great importance. A good number of language teachers feel unsure about using a tape recorder or a slide projector, and may never have used an overhead projector. A head of centre who perceives the need for the tutor to need these will also need to ensure that there are no hindrances to their use in terms of movement, accessibility and so on, once the tutor has indicated a readiness to try them. There should also be, of course, consultation about what sort of equipment to buy if money is available - here questions of compatibility, robustness and suitability for the linguists' needs should be discussed and, if need be, advice sought.

There are a variety of activities which can be arranged by a centre, in addition to the classes themselves. That these are popular is shown by the number of people who attend them when they are put on. The sorts of events which can be organised include residential weekends, intensive courses for two or three days, single language of cultural days and exchanges. There is no space here to go into the detailed organisation which is necessary. A first step would be to contact a centre which has organised such an event and ask advice. What one then needs to do is to gather round one a small group of tutors who can together plan activities which will, above all, allow people to speak the language during the day. The day should include, of course, a national lunch, some element of choice in the programme for participants, as well as contact with native speakers. Trying out your foreign language on a foreign national is an important feature. Through local twinning associations, individual or area connections, through organisations facilitating foreign contacts, a great deal of benefit can accrue to students who have, in many cases, only met foreigners on a camp site or at a hotel. It is usually very difficult for individual learners to arrange closer contact with foreigners than this and they do need a tutor in charge or the head of centre to help them in this goal.

(The Centre for Information on Language Teaching and Research, whose address appears at the front of this book, has publications giving advice as to how residential courses may be set up.)

A student home to home exchange

An example is given here of a successful exchange between the Merton Institute of Adult Education and the Volkshochschule in Montabaur in the Federal Republic of Germany. The visit was organised by Sheila Procter who is Tutor in Charge of Modern Languages, part of whose report is given here.

'Inspired by the enthusiasm of my students for exchange with Germans, I set about finding a suitable institute in Germany. The Central Bureau for Educational Visits and Exchanges had nothing on their books, but gave me the address of a German Volkshochschulverband and the strong advice that to follow up any personal contacts was more likely to produce quick results.

I had contact with a Gymnasium (Grammar School) teacher in Montabaur, a pleasant town near Koblenz and not too far to travel, so decided to try my luck there. I soon received an enthusiastic letter from one of her colleagues who was also a part-time adult education teacher. I decided to go ahead, so we obtained official backing.

Setting up the Exchange   Fortunately our interests were identical:
1) The most important aspect of the exchange would be the opportunity to stay in students' houses - but not a direct student-to-student exchange, as some of our students wanted to host, but were unable to travel to Germany, and vice versa.
2) We decided to fix a charge of £30 each to contribute to the hosts' expenses and group activities. This, with flight and insurance made a total cost of just under £100.
3) Each of us was to be responsible for the programme in the home country, the time to be shared between the family and group activities so that students also had time to share experiences and to meet other German hosts.
4) The visits were to last five days - as long as most adults wanted to be away from their families.
5) Details of family, age, job and interests should be sent so that as suitable a match as possible could be found.
6) There would be no programme of formal teaching. The aims were to put into practice in real situations what had already been learned, and to give an insight into German life.

The students   The group of twelve British students was varied; some had never been abroad before, the rest had never been other than as tourists.'

As can be seen from this short account such exchanges can be arranged without official help; the cost need not be great, and the students are given a quite unique personal experience of really meeting their counterparts. Often, as occurred in this case, continued contact and return visits can result.

Help can of course be obtained from a number of agencies. The Local Authority Education Department may have links or advice to give and tutors should also turn to the Central Bureau for Educational Visits and Exchanges, Seymour Mews House, Seymour Mews, London SW1.

HEADS OF CENTRE AND AREA LIAISON

It would be very desirable in non-urban areas particularly, where centres may not be able to provide a full range of levels in one language, for centres to co-ordinate provision. Heads of centre and community staff can do this if they wish, and can plan publicity together over a number of centres. Language classes do need to be looked on differently to other classes because of their sequential nature. It is possible in many subjects to have people with different levels of knowledge working side by side; it is difficult to achieve this in languages to the satisfaction of students, and mixed ability classes should be avoided. Any means which can be found to give students the sequential courses they look for should be explored, and co-ordination at least of information and advice between neighbouring centres is one of these means. This may mean heads of centre and teachers from two or three centres meeting to discuss courses. In part, this is a co-ordinating function appropriate to the Area Further Education Officers or whoever is responsible for local organisation, but there is no reason why some combined enrolment evenings or liaison meetings relating to enrolment should not be organised by heads of centre themselves.

Sometimes quite simple adjustments can be made which are helpful - as, for example, in urban areas particularly, arranging classes mutually so that all Level 1 classes in the area do not occur on the same night. This may then lead to more thorough discussion about organisation over a number of centres to achieve a full coverage and to try to cater for students such as the following unfortunate: 'This year I shall go out again and look for a second year German class.... and I suppose if I do find one it will then start all over again when I want a third year class. You get the feeling you will be 60 or 70 before you are anywhere near fluent.' (7)

It is true that adults will often wish to continue with a tutor they know, and that this, combined with the need to provide beginners classes can lead to the creation of mixed level classes. There are, however, many students who would like to be able to carry on, and for whom mixed level classes are very much a second best. As one put it, 'When you meet up with people who don't know any it's a bit off-putting'. (7) Such students should be able to locate a continuation course if one exists. It is a great pity when two potential classes in the same locality collapse through lack of take-up, when one combined class could succeed.

Area liaison is also important for more intensive courses, language days and so on. On such occasions students from a variety of centres come together and so, of course, publicity should be widely distributed - and contributions of help similarly.

Local liaison can also help to provide courses at different times of day in different centres. Because of the employment situation and perhaps too as a general trend, daytime courses for people who are not senior citizens are becoming more popular. Within areas such growth points can be noted and a combined programme discussed to use the best venues, 'flying tutors' and twilight times to some advantage.

RESUME

We have seen that, in order for the student to be properly provided for, a combination of the talents of the tutor and the head of centre is required. We have seen how this includes publicity, organising advice to the potential students, arranging meetings, stimulation of teachers, co-ordination of language courses, links

with other centres, as well as the normal function of providing as
adequate conditions as possible for the teaching and learning. One
senses, at times, a certain diffidence on the part of heads of
centre about assuming these various roles in relation to the tutors
and in liaising with other centres; such diffidence may be misplaced
as heads of centres are in a key position in relation to the profes-
sionalisation of the adult tutor and certainly have an in-service
education function to perform. By careful organisation the professional concern of the head of centre can be institutionalised so as
to achieve continuing staff development.

PART 2: IN-SERVICE EDUCATION

Throughout the country courses for tutors of languages are quite
insufficient and although there are courses of a general nature in
some areas there are fewer specifically language teaching
methodology courses. In part this is due to the lack of trainers,
but in part it is still due to the amateur status which is accorded
to adult education. Now, clearly, teaching a language is not an
amateur business. Done well it demands skills of a high order, -
inter-personal skills, organisational skills, creative skills, and a
degree of synthesising insight. It also demands knowledge of theory
and constant thought about how the theories may be applicable and
how they may be turned to practical use in one's own classroom.
Quite certainly, if the adult tutor of languages is to be regarded
as a professional then training, both initial and in-service is
called for. The need is sufficient for a case to be made for this to
be compulsory. It is not impossible over a period of years for an
LEA to require attendance on courses for all those who teach or wish
to teach languages to adults. Any initial reluctance on the part of
tutors at this compulsion seems to be replaced by enjoyment of the
opportunity to meet each other and to confront the problems which
face them, if experience in Leicestershire is anything to go by,
where there has now been an in-service requirement for five years.
If the tutors of languages do wish to be regarded as professionals,
then training must be seen as a priority and if it is to be effective, then LEA's will have to make this a requirement or give some
major incentive to tutors to participate.

Clearly there will be some who would wish to continue to train vol-
untarily. Is it worth requiring someone who teaches only one-and-a-
half or two hours per week to undergo in-service education? As in
the case of nursing, where there was a considerable opposition to
training at one time, the question must be looked at from the point
of view of the patient. The answer, in the view of the writer, then
becomes much clearer. It must be remembered that very many adult
tutors have had no training whatsoever in language teaching and have
only their own school experience to go on. This is quite obviously
insufficient, for apart from the fact that studying a subject does

not teach you how to convey it to another person, there is the like-
lihood that the experience pre-dates much recent knowledge and
development. There is, therefore, a need for courses for reasons of
quality in the service as a whole and in terms of professionalism
for the tutor; there is also a need because of the rate of progress
and change in the theoretical background to language learning and
the effect which this has continually on methodology and materials.
Language methodology changes over the years and various schools
arise - noted in the chapter by Shelagh Rixon - but what we have
seen in the last few years is a change of a very significant nature
in the analysis of language and in attention to how humans actually
behave towards each other using speech. This has concentrated
attention on a learner's performance needs rather than on the
student's study of the language itself. This is a very fundamental
shift and has led to gaps in knowledge at various levels in the
teaching process; there are knowledge gaps between the theorists and
the writers, between the writers and the teachers and all of us are
searching for a methodology, which adequately combines a functional
analysis of language with the grammatical systems which exist in a
language. Our methodology hitherto may be criticised for emphasising
the learning about the language, without leading to a rapid enough
acquisition and oral performance by the learner. Our modern
languages tutors need discussion, workshops and information in order
to keep up to date with continuing developments and to contribute to
them; to look at their own behaviour in terms of its effectiveness.

WHAT FORM SHOULD IN-SERVICE EDUCATION TAKE?

The balance of specific and general courses

In many parts of the country general courses are offered, and in
many cases these are a requirement. Such courses are concerned with
the adult student in a general sense, rather than methodology of a
specific subject. They are concerned with sociology, psychology, the
relationship between tutor and student, student participation in the
learning/teaching process and so on. In this publication we are
concerned with the specific needs of the tutors of languages and one
may ask in this connection whether sufficient attention is being
paid to the balance between general and specific training. Language
tutors do have needs in terms of methodology which are in some
respects similar to those of, say, a photography tutor or any other
- this is undeniable. But in large areas they are not similar. It is
also quite clear that many of these common things can be dealt with
in relation to the work which goes on in the language class. This
partly subject-oriented perspective is necessary, as clearly a
tutor's relationship with the class will vary from subject to
subject. The very best language teaching to adults will always have
an element of dependence on the teacher by the students, which is
greater than the dependence found in many subjects. The field for

independent action, experimentation and application of ideas by students is clearly much wider in design based subjects, for example, than in languages. And if we take the example of sociology, then the contribution which students can make is considerable, and the tutor him or herself will clearly have to behave very differently in the classroom to the tutor of the language class. The language tutors need to spend time in their in-service courses looking at the element of student involvement with specific reference to language teaching and learning. This needs to see constantly how a particular unit of work can be made accessible to students and what particular techniques will help in this. It is difficult to see how any other than very general techniques can be conveyed from other subject areas. This is not to deny that some general course experience is essential, and nothing said here is meant to detract from the issues confronted in such courses, such as co-operation, critical thinking, personal development and tutor/-student relationships - but equally it needs to be said that for a language tutor these courses are by far not sufficient alone and will be of little direct help to the tutor in his or her task of teaching languages.

Another reason for raising this point is the amount of time available in relation to the fairly considerable learning load which faces the tutor in a language methodology course. The potential teacher of languages to adults may, depending on experience, have to readjust his or her perspective quite considerably from a school-based one. There will also be a need to reflect on the sort of language teaching one had oneself and how far this has influenced one's view of what language teaching is all about. But in addition to this there is a considerable learning load of new terminology and an exploration of new ideas and analyses of language and syllabus design, course progression and so on, and such new or different views have to be turned into practical realisation. Time is required for this. Time is required for intellectually perceived concepts to be really integrated into classroom practice, in terms of materials, methods and approaches to students. The degree to which the teachers knowledge and ability in the language is mediated to the students is the measure of his or her success, and many of the most crucial skills involved in this process require time, reflection and practice.

The basic elements for a course for tutors

Clearly tutors' experience and knowledge vary and there is not space here to develop fully the detailed content of a course. Such has been done very well elsewhere - for example, by the RSA and by the International Certificate Conference. (9 and 10) However, the main elements of a course should include discussion and practical work on the following themes:

1. The tutor and the class
1.1. Teaching adult students
   - who they are;
   - what positive things adults may bring to a class and what inhibitions they may also have;
   - what effects schooling may have;
   - students' experience of the educational world and its rather special vocabulary;
   - what effect ageing may have.
1.2. School-based attitudes
   - contrast school and adult needs;
   - authority relationships, our view of the teacher, the tutor and the class;
   - purposes in learning;
   - voluntariness and compulsion;
   - attitudes to marking, assessment and a tutor's judgement.
1.3. Motivation
   - why adults like to go to evening classes;
   - what their expectations are;
   - whether expectations fit the offering;
   - whether expectations are real.
1.4. Classroom relationships
   - types of seating arrangement, their effect or purpose;
   - inter-student relationships;
   - the difficult student;
   - social class differences.
1.5. Drop-out
   - why students go away;
   - how it may be mitigated.
1.6. Observation
   - visiting language classes with a guide as to what to look for;
   - discussion of observation in terms of relationships, use of the foreign language, type of material, pace, activities, participation, atmosphere, etc.

2. A look at language
2.1. Language awareness exercises;
2.2. Experience of learning a language;
2.3. A study of language showing a variety of systems;
2.4. A comparison of syllabus types;
2.5. An introduction to functional analysis and practice of it;
2.6. A discussion of the relationships between grammatical and functional analysis.

3. Language needs of students
3.1. How these may be expressed and described;
3.2. The time available for a course; consequences of this;
3.3. Discussion of units to include a course;
3.4. Description of a course; writing of publicity.

4. Unit design
4.1. Discussion of units to include in a course;
4.2. Selection of a unit and analysis of it in terms of:
   - functions, notions;
   - possible exponents to be used;
   - possible exponents to be understood;
   - modes of language use;
   - cultural overtones, differences, etc;
4.3. Editing of the language produced for a unit.

5. Methodology
5.1. Using the unit which has been worked on
   - analysis of it in terms of priorities and objectives;
   - discussion of communication and meaning;
   - analysis of possible types of materials needed;
   - step by step discussion of methodology, hand in hand
     with the creation of materials and the analysis of
     existing contributing materials;
   - techniques for encouraging speech, communicative activities,
     group work, etc;
   - questioning techniques and the reduction of stress in
     the learners;
   - use of items of equipment as needed or suggested by the
     methodology;
   - trying the materials out.

6. Other
   - the course should include a discussion of language days,
     intensive courses, links with twinning associations, etc.

It is not suggested that a course should always proceed in this way.
However, the main elements of the course are set out here, some of
which will certainly recur throughout the period of training in
different guises or with different emphases. Elements from Section 1
above would certainly constantly recur. Nor does the way in which
the suggestions are set out above give any idea of the amount of
time each part should take. By far the largest slice of time is,
however, inevitably given up to the discussion and devising of
syllabus and to working on materials. Such practical work is
absolutely essential and throws light on much of the earlier and
later discussions.

The question is sometimes raised as to why participants need to go
through the process of developing a unit of work, as there are
course books available which do the job. The purpose, in the
writer's view, is to help students go through the processes of
evaluation, selection and editing so that they will be able to look
at course books, etc, as a source of materials to be used
selectively in a variety of ways, rather than as a corpus of
knowledge all of which must be 'covered'.

The nature of a course

The manner in which an in-service course is conducted is in itself a
lesson to participants and, towards its end, it is worth discussing
their experience of the course so that they can objectively assess
their experience. It is also a good idea to ask participants at the
beginning of a course what they would like it to contain and then,
in discussion with them, develop the themes which the course might
cover. It is likely that many of the themes suggested above will be
brought forward, but the important thing is that students should
themselves realise from the beginning that courses are processes of
discovery arising from needs and desires rather than the passive
imbibing of others' ideas. The course itself, therefore, should be a
demonstration of good practice, from which participants can learn.

It has often been noted that if people are taught in a directive
manner, they appear less bright and inventive than when they are
allowed to participate and create ideas and contribute for themselves. They certainly derive little satisfaction from long periods
of sitting and listening (which is perhaps why it is sometimes so
tiring). So from two points of view it is important that any in-
service course should be participatory – firstly, the course itself
is a powerful demonstration of how to proceed with people, and
secondly, it is more enjoyable and productive if there is participation. This point is well made in Foreign language teaching in
adult education; a teacher training manual of the International
Certificate Conference. (10) 'An important element in this initial
training programme is its emphasis on learning by doing, or communication, interaction and self-discovery techniques. This is not only
propagated as desirable teaching practice, but is built into the
whole training programme as exemplary of a pedagogic and didactic
methodology suitable for adult education' (p 11).

A further necessary aspect is to ensure that the content and the
conditions of the course are in harmony with the conditions under
which the participants will have to work. This perhaps strengthens
the point about the practical nature of such courses and the neces-
sity of ensuring that participants' voices are heard in the
selection of items for study and development. The object of any
course must be to create an awareness of the process involved from
the language learners' point of view. In order to attain such
awareness participants need time to reflect on their experience.
They also need to receive theoretical input at the time and point
where they are required in order to help solve the problem or to
clarify a puzzle. For this reason again participatory courses are
valuable as they allow people more chance of progression at their
own rate.

Courses run in this way have more chance of bringing participants to
the point of wanting to learn about a new field or perspective and

wanting to question their own point of view otherwise 'un des
dangers (est de) remplacer sans plus d'analyse un modèle pédagogique
par un autre, (et) il semble parfaitement superflu de plaquer des
contenus nouveaux sur des pratiques anciennes sans que ces pratiques
aient été elle-mêmes revues sérieusement'. (11)

To mitigate this problem the EFL courses run by the Bell School of
Languages interestingly include feedback after a period when participants have had time to reflect for, say, six months on their
experience and to apply it, integrating it into their own manner of
proceeding. Such an arrangement would be possible for LEAs. It may
also be that courses, which run over a period of weeks with once-
weekly meetings, perhaps including occasional days, have a more
long-lasting effect than those which seek to work intensively, pre-
cisely because there is time to reflect and work on the experiences
of each session.

RESUME

In this section on in-service education and in the preceding section
dealing with organisation the argument has been put forward that a
more professional view should be taken of the job of the tutor, of
the tutor's relationship to the head of centre and of the role of
the head of centre. There does seem little doubt that most tutors
value discussion and the chance this brings to compare notes and to
learn from others about what they are doing. The size of the adult
education programme certainly warrants it, as does the need nationally for a more systematic provision and opportunity for people,
practically whose only access to this skill is through the medium of
the adult education institution.

REFERENCES

(1) Advisory Council for Adult and Continuing Education: Protecting
     the future for adult education. Advisory Council for Adult and
     Continuing Education, 1981, p 19, para. 13.

(2) Sidwell, D M: 'A survey of modern language classes.' Adult
     Education, vol 52, no. 5, January 1980.

(3) Rybak, S: 'Learning languages for the BBC.' Research into
     courses for adults. BBC, 1980.

(4) Sidwell, D M: 'The local education authority and the adult
     learner of languages.' British Journal of Language Teaching,
     vol 8, nos. 2 and 3, winter 1980, p 197.

(5) A prospectus from the General Education Department of the
     Loughborough Technical College.

(6) See (5) above.

(7) See (2) above.

(8) Protecting the future for adult education. See (1) above. p 36
     para. 7.

(9) Royal Society of Arts: Teaching practice and teacher-training
     materials. (Report on the Conference on RSA Certificate TEFL
     courses, Nonington, 1980.) Hilderstone International, Broad-
     stairs, Kent, 1980.

(10) Thomas, G W and J Ferentzi-Sheppard (eds): Foreign language
     teaching in adult education. A teacher training manual. (The
     International Certificate Conference.) Pädagogische Arbeits-
     stelle des D.V.V., Holzhausenstrasse 21, 6000 Frankfurt-Main.

(11) Council for Cultural Co-operation: Modern languages compendium
     of teacher training programmes. (Draft copy.) Council of
     Europe, September 1981, p 9.

PUBLIC EXAMINATIONS AND ACHIEVEMENT TESTS

Lynn Jones and Alan Moys

It is well known among those concerned with teaching languages to adults that the learners are a very diverse group: diverse not only in their previous knowledge and experience of language learning, but also in their aims and expectations. Some (perhaps a majority) join language classes in order to learn as much of a language as they need for holiday or travel; while others may see their language course as a step, in terms of qualification, towards an eventual academic goal. Whatever their motivation, a significant proportion of learners respond positively to the idea of undergoing some form of external test to measure their achievement.

For the new teacher of languages to adults, the choice of examination/test styles and levels is bewildering. This chapter is intended to provide some indication of the choices available, concentrating on the more elementary levels. In all cases, teachers requiring more detailed information should write direct to the bodies concerned (see address list at the end of this chapter). In particular, it should be remembered that examination regulations and syllabus content may change from one year to the next, so up-to-date literature is essential.

Before embarking on a more detailed exploration of the field, two important areas need consideration: 'school' examinations, and choice of languages.

'School' examination

This section refers particularly to the General Certificate of Education (GCE) examinations. While the other 16+ examination, the Certificate of Secondary Education (CSE) is only available to school pupils, it is, in fact, strictly incorrect to describe the GCE as a school examination, since it is available to candidates of all ages. Since GCE gives single-subject certification, adult learners may envisage taking it at Ordinary or Advanced level in the language of their choice. The principle advantage of so doing is that GCE represents a widely accepted academic qualification, and is a requirement for entry into many advanced courses and as a career qualification in many fields.

Viewed purely as a foreign language examination, however, GCE may not be the most appropriate target for adult centre learners. It is designed to assess performance after 5 years of school study (500-600) hours; it has hitherto placed considerable emphasis in most cases on written language, and has been more insistent on formal accuracy than on communicative effectiveness. For a detailed exploration of syllabuses, approaches to marking and assessment, etc, at GCE Ordinary level, teachers are referred to Modern languages examination at 16+: a critical analysis (Moys, Page, Harding and Printon), CILT, 1981.

The development in school of Graded Tests as part of the Graded Objectives approach to language testing aims at prividing an alternative system which enables learners kto be tested on their achievement in particular language ski8lls (reading, speaking, listening, for example) at different levels and throughout their course rather than only at the end. Teachers of adult students might consider these schemes, information and advice being available from Local Authority Languages Advisers or from the Centre for Information on Language Teaching and Research, 20 Carlton House Terrace, London SW1Y 5AP.

CHOICE OF LANGUAGES

For teachers of French, German, and Spanish the choice of examining bodies is very wide. All the examinations listed in this chapter are available for these languages, often at a variety of levels.

Italian and Russian are offered by a smaller number of bodies. Other languages (such as Portuguese, Arabic, Japanese, Gujarati) are mainly available from two examining sources, the Institute of Linguists (write for details) and at GCE 'O' level, through the following GCE boards: London, Oxford, Cambridge, the Joint Matriculation Board and the Associated Examining Board.

The Institute of Linguists

The Institute of Linguists offers a range of examinations from the Preliminary Certificate up to the Final Diploma. The syllabuses are designed for adults, include no literature or literary texts, and give full and useful information on the tests and the way in which they are assessed. The comments given here relate to the Preliminary Certificate and the Grade I Certificate only; students and teachers looking for a suitable examination for post-'O' level study might well consider the Grade II Certificate as an alternative to GCE Advanced Level syllabuses.

1) The Preliminary Certificate, consisting of oral tests, aural comprehension and general knowledge of the country, contains no examination of writing in the foreign language. The oral tests, a conversation and a situational role-play, relate to personal interests of the candidate - 'my holidays', 'my district or town', 'a book, play or film' - and to everyday contexts such as travel agency, or a post office. Assessment criteria focus on understanding

and resourcefulness in making oneself understood; the Institute recognises that the language used at this level is likely to be 'rudimentary and defective'. Such an attitude will be welcomed by many teachers as well as by the candidates themselves. The aural comprehension follows the convention of a spoken text with questions to be answered in English, though the text is described as 'simple and practical'.

The general knowledge test to be answered in short note form is often a source of anxiety since the items are entirely unpredictable – a common idiom, the name of a national dish, a writer, place or building or a national custom. Presumably this test is designed to reflect the sort of items that are covered in the course materials used, but it can lead to a considerable amount of specific teaching – in English because of the nature of this test – for this part of the examination carries as many marks as the oral and the aural comprehension.

2) The Grade I Certificate of the Institute of Linguists contains an oral examination similar to, but more demanding than at Preliminary level and the aural comprehension test includes dictation. Assessment criteria of oral task still give credit to confidence and resourcefulness, demanding a standard of accuracy that would allow a native speaker to 'understand readily'. The written tests at this level include written comprehension, translation into English, and a choice of two tests of writing in the foreign language – a letter or short article, and general knowledge of the country, a very wide-ranging though generous choice of topics. This Certificate is often regarded as the 'equivalent' of '0' level and does indeed contain a similar range of language skills and tests, but the language, tests and situations are not literary in style or register, but relate to everyday life and more adult interests than is commonly the case at '0' level.

The Royal Society of Arts

An interesting development is the Preliminary Level Examination being developed by the Royal Society of Arts, the explanatory booklet for which is more than just a syllabus. It contains descriptions of the examination, and examples of the types of tests used, full details of levels of performance and assessment criteria and an extremely useful section on suggestions for the linguistic content of syllabus. Guidelines on grammatical items to be developed for receptive and productive purposes are thorough and helpful; many teachers making the transition from the grammar/translation method of teaching will welcome in particular the advice in the publication referring to French on what need not be taught.

The examinations are designed for learners after 50-60 hours of study, though they may also be very suitable for adults on a 'refresher course'. The tests are confined to listening, reading and conversation skills and use tasks that are described as 'communicative in nature that resemble the sort of real life demands made on those who visit a foreign country'. Every attempt has been made to use authentic material for the listening and reading tests. They genuinely test understanding - ticking a range of facilities offered by a hotel, marking a cross on a map after listening to directions, or writing a letter in English in response to a letter in the foreign language which asks for several pieces of specific information, a far more authentic and valid test of understanding than, for example, a translation.

The oral tests - conversations, guided translations and situational conversations - concentrate on asking for and giving information, transacting everyday affairs and making plans and decisions. What is unusual about this oral examination is that the teacher is involved in the tasks not as the examiner but as a 'native speaker trying to help the candidate to understand and express things', while the examiner observes and assesses. This idea should do much to reduce stress and artificiality and should enable good classroom practice to be extended more naturally into the examination itself.

For all parts of the examination, clear information is given about the purpose of the tasks, what is expected from the candidate, and the meaning of the grades to be awarded. The use of a Profile showing performance standards in the three sections of the examination will enable students to see their own strengths and weaknesses rather than receive one aggregated mark or grade.

These examinations are now available in French, German, Spanish and Italian, at Level I. Further levels will be available later. Meanwhile, the well-established Stage I, II and III examinations, based on structural principles, continue to be available. The difference of emphasis is clearly indicated by this extract from the existing Stage I description: 'Stage I aims to test comprehension of spoken and written language, production of connected prose or letter, translation into English, reading aloud and conversing in the language.... Grammatical accuracy is important.'

The London Chamber of Commerce and Industry

The Commercial Education Scheme of the LCCI has developed the FLIC (Foreign Language for Industry and Commerce) examination scheme. These tests, which have the advantage of being available to candidates at any time of the year, are primarily tests of speaking and listening. There are no written tests. The four examinations progress from Elementary (twenty-minute test with conversation, carrying out instructions, a presentation in the foreign language of a special subject or topic, reading, summary on the foreign language of an English text and of a recorded conversation).

The LCCI also continues to offer examinations in the popular languages at Elementary, Intermediate and Higher Levels, all involving the more traditional tests of written translation, reading comprehension with answers in the foreign language, and essay or letter writing.

The Pitman Examinations Institute

Examinations are offered at three levels (Elementary, Intermediate and Advanced), in French, German and Spanish. The examinations are unusual in that, while the syllabus booklet clearly and persuasively argues for listening and speaking to have top priority, followed by reading, with writing of least importance, and with an emphasis on communication, the examination tests do not include oral assessment. The other three areas (listening, reading and writing) are tested through a range of activities (listening comprehension with questions in English, reading comprehension with questions in the foreign language and in English, communication (as opposed to translation) of factual matter from English through written foreign language, and (at the higher levels) summary writing (English and the foreign language).

BBC Achievement Tests

Perhaps the most significant feature of the adult foreign language learning scene in the United Kingdom over the past twenty years has been the contribution of the BBC in developing multi-media programmes (television, radio, records/cassettes, book material) for would-be learners of a range of languages. These programmes are widely used in adult education and by home learners. For the more recently produced series, the BBC has arranged with independent examining bodies for the availability of achievement tests for learners, closely related in content and activity to the course being followed. It is interesting that the term achievement tests is used, since it reflects a determination in the devising of the tests to provide the learner with maximum encouragement to show what he can do rather than what he cannot. Achievement tests are available for 'Kontakte' and 'Ensemble' (from the University of Cambridge Local Examinations Syndicate), and for 'Digame' (from the Institute of Linguists).

Addresses

Institute of Linguists
Mangold House
24a Highbury Grove
London N5 2EA

London Chamber of Commerce and Industry
Commercial Education Scheme
Marlowe House
Station Road
Sidcup
Kent DA15 7BJ

Pitman Examinations Institute
Godalming
Surrey GU7 1UU

Royal Society of Arts Examinations Board
John Adam Street
Adelphi
London WC2N 6EZ

General Certification of Education (GCE) Examining Bodies

The Associated Examining Board for the General Certificate of
 Education
Wellington House
Aldershot
Hants GU11 1BQ

The Joint Matriculation Board
Manchester M15 6EU

The University Entrance and School Examinations Council
University of London
66/72 Gower Street
London WC1E 6EE

The Oxford Delegacy of Local Examinations
Department of Local Examinations
Ewert Place
Banbury Road
Summertown
Oxford OX2 7BZ

University of Cambridge Local Examinations Syndicate
Syndicate Buildings
17 Harvey Road
Cambridge CB1 2EU

CILT

**Centre for Information on
Language Teaching and Research**

provides

Modern Language Teachers

with

INFORMATION

on all aspects of modern language teaching - materials
methodology and research.

****

To: CILT, 20 Carlton House Terrace, London SW1Y

Please send me details of your information services and
publications.

NAME...

SCHOOL...

ADDRESS..

....